Wrestling for {REMOTE} Control

Nothing builds
togetherness like

Wrestling
for
{REMOTE}
Control

G. Ron Darbee

BROADMAN
&HOLMAN
PUBLISHERS

Nashville, Tennessee

Published by Broadman & Holman Publishers, Nashville, Tennessee
Acquisitions & Development Editor: Vicki Crumpton
Interior Design: Steven Boyd
Printed in the United States of America

4261-93
0-8054-6193-0

Dewey Decimal Classification: 248.4
Subject Heading: CHRISTIAN LIFE—HUMOR
Library of Congress Card Catalog Number: 96-7810

Unless otherwise noted, Scripture quotations are from the Holy Bible, New International Version, copyright © 1973, 1978, 1984 by International Bible Society.

Library of Congress Cataloging-in-Publication Data
Darbee, G. Ron, 1961–
    Wrestling for remote control / G. Ron Darbee.
    p.   cm.
    ISBN 0-8054-6193-0 (pbk.)
    1. Christian life—Humor. 2. Christian life—Anecdotes.
3. Darbee, G. Ron, 1961–.4. Christian life—Baptist authors.
    I. Title.
    BV4517.D37   1996
    248.4—dc20

    96-7810
    CIP

96 97 98 99 00 5 4 3 2 1

To my wife, Sue, and our children, Ron and Melissa.
Your love and humor brighten my life.

Contents

Acknowledgments

I would like to borrow from a time-worn cliché and mention that a book is never written without the help and support of many people. Actually a book of this sort is rarely written without several years of therapy and at least one major competency hearing. I assure you that I've managed to avoid both—so far.

I very much want to thank my wife, Susan, and our children, Ron and Melissa. These remain their stories as much as they are mine. Without my family, and their tolerance for exaggeration, this manuscript would have fit neatly on the back of a postcard. Also thanks to my parents for allowing me to survive adolescence despite their better judgment.

To Jerry Ruble and Steve Souza, the men who mentor and disciple me in my walk with God, thank you for your example and endless encouragement. To our pastors: Dennis Henderson, Bill Barnett, Frank Sanza, Dave Harris, and Dave Malouf, my appreciation for your service both to our Lord and

His people. Special thanks to Pastor Craig Stonehocker, my friend and the most transparent, down-to-earth disciple I have ever known.

I owe a great deal to Bob Haslam, retired minister and former editor of *Light and Life* magazine, who published my first submission. His constant encouragement and friendship continue to provide motivation. Also David Kopp, founding editor of *Parents of Teenagers*, among other magazines, for pushing me to improve my skills and helping me to see my work as a gift returned to God.

Finally, and with sincere gratitude, my thanks to Vicki Crumpton and the Broadman & Holman team for their partnership in this publication and for believing that humor has a place in our lives.

ONE

Wrestling for Control

"Aaaahhhhhh!" my son screamed as he lunged for the prize resting on the arm of the couch. I reacted quickly. A well-thrown hip-check sent his thin, athletic frame crashing into the love seat. The cat bolted from the room, knocking a candy dish to the floor as I sauntered to the couch to claim my reward.

"Give it to me, Dad." Ron (my namesake) scowled from his perch on the love seat.

"No," my voice totally composed.

"Dad, I want the remote."

"You're not ready." I dangled the controller between two fingers, taunting the poor boy. "You'd just point it at your mom and hit the mute button anyway."

"This is not cool," he warned.

I reacted as any father would, striking my best pose, flexing my biceps, triceps, and those softening orbs I used to call pecs. "No," I repeated. "Maybe when you're older."

"I'm not sitting through another night of 'Fishing with Earl,' Dad. You know I could take it if I wanted to. Don't make me hurt you."

A threat! Ron was feeling his oats. "Go ahead. Make my day," I said.

"Dad, nobody says that anymore. You are such a dweeb."

"Dweeb? A dweeb?" I questioned. "I wasn't a dweeb when you needed a learner's permit or car insurance. I was way cool as I recall. I wasn't a dweeb when you wanted money for those Michael Jackson, air-pump, glow-in-the-dark sneakers either."

"Michael Jordan, Dad."

"Jackson, Jordan, what's the difference?"

"Three feet and a white glove for starters. You're really losing it in your old age. Very uncool, Dad, even for a geezer."

"Well, it seems to me I was pretty cool when you and your friends needed a place to throw your party last weekend. 'This is really cool, Mr. Darbee,' 'You're great. I wish my parents were as cool as you, Mr. Darbee.' It seems there's been a change in tune. I know how we can settle this!" I said, the beginnings of an idea taking form. "I'll ask your friends what they think about all this. Wait, let me throw on my Bermuda shorts, a pair of black socks, and some sandals first, and we'll go conduct our little survey. I don't need a T-shirt, do I?"

"You wouldn't."

"I would."

"You'd better not."

"I will."

I made a mad dash for the door, but my son dove and caught me by a leg, holding on for life and reputation.

"Mom!" he yelled. "Dad's being a jerk!"

"That's no way to talk about your father," I reminded him, hobbling toward the door, but making little progress. "Should we start with the guys or the girls?" He grabbed my other leg, and I dropped to the floor to engage him in combat. "Wrestling match, is it?" I yelled, confident that I had the advantage in weight class. As we battled for position, I was determined that cunning and experience would not bow to youth and energy. Distracting him with the sounds of my joints cracking, I strategically blocked his flying-knee slam with my groin and cried out for his surrender.

"Had enough?" I screeched in a soprano that would bring tears to Twyla Paris's eyes. (A tear or two was forming in my own eyes as well.)

"Never." His efforts to appear fresh and ready to go didn't fool me. I knew he was wearing down.

In an attempt to build a false sense of confidence, I countered his knee slam by jamming my neck into his headlock. He was like putty in my hands, and there was nothing left but to wait and pretend that the lack of oxygen was getting to me.

Suddenly, the sound of a soft, feminine voice interrupted our horseplay.

"*Stop*! Stop it right now! You animals are going to destroy the entire house," Sue screamed. It was obvious by her subtle tones that she was concerned only for my well-being. "What are you lunatics trying to prove?"

"Just showing our boy some of my old college wrestling moves, Dear," I gasped, sucking oxygen from between the strands of carpet. "He's a real natural. In a couple of years he'll give me a run for my money."

"Really," she said. "Interesting move. In nursing school they call that suffocation. The blue lips tend to give it away."

From the corner of her eye she caught movement at my feet and mistakenly confused a muscle spasm for an attempt to brush pieces of candy dish under the love seat. "What is that?" she asked.

"What?" Ron and I responded in unison.

"Who broke my candy dish?"

"Oh, that. The cat did it," I explained. "Don't worry, Honey," I comforted. "It was pretty old anyway."

"It wasn't old. It was my grandmother's," she said, looking as if she might wrestle us both into submission. "I don't believe you two sometimes. You're always competing over something. What was it this time, a race for the last Oreo or just a show of strength? It's true, isn't it? Testosterone really does kill brain cells."

At the first sign of lip movement, I elbowed my son in the ribs, a signal that his mother's question was rhetorical. Sue left the room, shaking her head in disbelief and muttering something about future sleeping arrangements. I felt it would be inappropriate to ask her to help with the cleanup.

"What do we do now?" Ron asked.

"I suppose we could watch a little TV," I said, tossing him the remote. "Here, you try, but only the odd-numbered channels; you've got to start slow. And none of that MTV."

"Thanks, Dad," he said, settling into the love seat. "Hey, what did she mean about testosterone and brain cells?"

"Who?"

"Never mind, Dad. Never mind."

Fathers, do not exasperate your children; instead,
bring them up in the training and instruction of the Lord.

Ephesians 6:4

TWO

I Once Was Lost

$\mathbb{S}$pending some time alone with a group of boys may turn out to be the most satisfying experience of your life."

Thinking back on our youth pastor's words, I realize I may have been a little harsh when I referred to him as "that lying pagan." It's not as if he said "relaxing" or "pleasing" or "gratifying"; he said "satisfying." And I imagine that if you're twisted enough to become a youth pastor in the first place, you might be able to stretch your imagination to the point of calling the experience satisfying—satisfying in the same way that dislodging a fish hook from your index finger is satisfying, or removing your sneakers after running the Boston Marathon.

Greg's invitation to spend a weekend in the wilderness with ten fourth-grade boys was answered with something short of boundless elation on my part. Had it been just a simple invitation, I would have turned it down without a second thought. But his words sounded like a dare. My wife called it goading, but she is a bit cynical.

"Come on, Ron, they're just kids!" Greg said, going for the soft underbelly of masculine pride. "What can they possibly do to you?"

"Will you listen to yourself!" I said. "Don't you remember Arlo Wilson? He wasn't always a tenor, you know!"

"He's not much of a tenor now," Greg said.

"That's not the point! They did that to him. They changed him."

"Well, Ron, if you're afraid—"

"Just hold on a minute," I said. "It's not like I'm scared or anything, it's just that—"

"No, Ron, really. I can ask Lewis," he said. "Maybe we can find an area of service that would better suit you. Say, the choir robes are looking a little worn. Do you sew, by chance?"

"Now that's it," I demanded. "You're just going to have to find yourself another seamstress, Pastor. I'm going camping with those boys."

Sue stood at my side throughout the conversation, trying to remember where she stashed my backpack and sleeping bag. Call it women's intuition or just a mean streak, but she claimed to have known the outcome from the start.

"Pretty deft maneuvering, Einstein," she said, as we pulled away from the church. "By my estimation, you lasted all of two and a half minutes. A new record, I believe."

"Thank you, Dear. It's always nice to know I have your support."

Over the next two weeks, transportation arrangements were made, permission slips signed, and prayer networks established. My own prayer, offered up each morning, was simple and to the point. "Dear God, please watch over me as I venture into this madness. Keep me safe and healthy, and help me to bring home a respectable percentage of the boys that I start out with."

D Day arrived, and, following the age-old tradition of rising at some ridiculously early hour before embarking on a journey, we departed. The bus ride to the mountains was uneventful, the boys passing time with a few ageless camp songs and a story or two. Sandwiches provided by the women's Bible study group were devoured en route, and I began to feel somewhat at ease. Maybe this wasn't going to be so bad after all.

Looking back with 20/20 hindsight, I realize it was at this point I should have been most concerned. Ten-year-old boys are notorious for their ability to lull you into a false sense of security. However, my mind somewhat dull for lack of sleep, I failed to recognize the warning signs. Our driver pulled into the staging area of Shadow Mountain Wilderness Refuge, and ten and a half smiles exited the bus.

"Listen up," I instructed. "Grab your packs and sleeping bags, and form two lines by the trail, smallest boys in front. Yes, Alex?" I asked in response to a waving hand.

"How long will we have to walk?"

"About an hour," I replied. "From the looks of the map that Pastor Greg gave us, our campsite is about four miles in."

"Will there be Nintendo?" questioned another boy.

"No, no video games."

"Do they have cable?"

"No, there isn't any cable. There isn't even any 'they.' This is the wilderness!" I said, exasperated by the barrage of questions. "What is it, Matthew?" I growled at a youth, standing on tiptoe, waving his arm like a surrender flag.

"We used to have cable, but my dad didn't want it anymore."

"Enough with the cable already! Can we get on the trail before the Lord calls us home?"

"When is the Lord gonna call us home?" asked yet another boy.

"Soon, soon. Before I'm institutionalized, I'd like to think. Now get moving," I cried, and hurried the little mob toward the trail.

As we walked, I lost all track of time. Minutes seemed like hours as the tranquillity of nature was interrupted by the complaints of the boys: "Emilio's stepping on the back of my shoes!" "My feet hurt," and chorus after chorus of the ever popular "Are we there yet?" A glance at my watch gave me the first indication we might have strayed from our planned route.

"Does anyone remember coming to a fork in the trail?" I asked, trying to keep any hint of distress from my voice.

"I do," answered Alex.

"How far back was it?"

"I don't know."

"Wonderful. Your parents must be very proud. Does anyone else remember a fork?" weariness beginning to tell in my voice.

"I have a Power Ranger fork at home," volunteered Matthew.

"Let's head back this way for a while, and keep your eyes peeled for a fork in the path," I directed.

Two hours passed, and it was becoming noticeably quiet in the ranks. I called the group to a stop, and we set down to ponder our situation. Emilio and two others were perched on a fallen tree, giving fresh lyrics to old gospel tunes.

"I once was found, but now am lost—" sang the trio.

"Boys, I don't believe that is helping," I said. "Besides, I'm sure we'll find our way back to the right path soon. God won't let us wander around out here forever."

"God made the Israelites wander in the desert for forty years," whined Stewart. "You don't think we'll be here for forty years, do you?"

"No way," chided Emilio. "Mr. Ron would be dead by then."

"Emilio, much as I hate to disappoint you, there's a good chance that I may well be alive for another forty years, though I wouldn't give my mental faculties that many minutes. Anyway, I'm sure we'll all be just fine."

"Maybe we should pray or something," offered Alex.

"That's a good idea, Alex. Would you like to lead us?"

"OK. Dear heavenly Father, this is Alex. We love You and know You really love us back. Please take good care of us, and help Mr. Ron figure out where we are. Keep us safe, and don't let us get eaten by any bears or lions or stuff. And God, if we don't find the path real soon, please let Mr. Ron take us to McDonald's for dinner. Amen."

"That was just fine, Alex. Don't count on McDonald's though," I smiled, tousling his matted hair.

"Why not? We've been walking a long time, and I'm getting real hungry."

"Alex," I said, kneeling down to reason with the boy, "I know you're tired and hungry, but we're probably miles from the nearest fast-food restaurant."

"Nuh-uh," he replied, pointing past my shoulder. "There's one right over there."

"Over where?" I asked, dumbfounded.

"Through the trees," he responded, still pointing. "You can see the arches if you stand on that log."

Not sure if I should hug the child or just throw him for distance, I stood quietly for a moment, practicing some breathing techniques recalled from my days as a Lamaze coach.

"Alex," I asked, fighting to keep the smile on my face and my hands in my pockets. "Why didn't you tell me there was a McDonald's over there?"

"I didn't know you were looking for one. Is it near our campsite?"

A polite young man in a paper hat set us back on course, and we pitched camp for what turned out to be a wonderful—if somewhat less eventful—weekend. Bonds were formed and friendships strengthened. Boys learned the value of fellowship, and I may have learned a thing or two about a servant's heart.

The ride home was quiet, the troops a little subdued from the weekend's activities. We pulled into the church parking lot to the waves and shouts of parents and siblings. Pastor Greg clasped my shoulder as I collected my gear.

"Looks like things went pretty well."

"Not bad, really," I responded. "I feel kind of good about the whole thing."

"I knew you would," Greg replied. "Now next year—"

"Hold on," I said, backing into the side of the bus. "I don't think I'll be involved next year."

"Nonsense. Remember, 'He who began a good work in you will carry it on to completion.' I was just thinking, have you done any deep-sea fishing?"

Whatever you do, work at it with all your heart,
as working for the Lord, not for men, since you know that you will
receive an inheritance from the Lord as a reward.
It is the Lord Christ you are serving.

Colossians 3:23–24

THREE

Brooklyn's Answer to King Solomon

Regardless of our backgrounds, we have all shared the experience of having a friend who was light-years ahead of the pack. You remember, the wonderful little child who couldn't wait to break the news about Santa Claus and the Easter bunny, or maybe the facts of life. Armed with no more than 10 percent of the truth, this kid's mind was a blunt instrument, poised to bludgeon the bits and pieces of childhood we were desperately clinging to. In my neighborhood, this role was filled by Anthony Gianelli, or Tony G., as he preferred to be called.

I looked up to Tony. We all did. There wasn't a topic in the world that he couldn't discuss and very few on which he wasn't an outright expert. At the ripe old age of eleven, Anthony Gianelli had achieved virtual stardom on our block. And for all practical purposes, our block was the entire world.

Tony was Brooklyn's answer to King Solomon, Thomas Edison, and Albert Einstein all rolled up into one. I was well into my teen years before I had convinced myself that I knew everything. Tony G. didn't have to wait for adolescence.

After several indepth conversations with Tony, I realized that my parents' education had failed to provide them with some of the finer details of many topics. The thought crossed my mind that they had intentionally neglected to discuss these points with me. But more than likely, they just didn't have the benefit of Tony's insight.

It was Anthony who explained to me how dirt formed a protective layer over your skin, thus reducing the risk of disease. More than once, I tried to persuade him to come home with me and share this wisdom with my parents, but he never had the time, what with the heavy demands on his schedule and all.

The majority of the adults in our neighborhood held Tony in somewhat less than high regard. If the truth be known, they out-and-out disliked him. But just as a prophet is not welcome in his own land, neither is a great child intellect on his home turf. My parents appeared split on the subject. My mother counseled me to stay clear of "that boy," and my father constantly mentioned how he just couldn't wait until he had a chance to spend some time alone with him.

"If I had just ten minutes alone with the little urchin, I'd be a happy man," my dad would say, his left eyebrow twitching strangely.

As unbelievable as it might seem, young Gianelli played an important part in my initial decision to learn more about the Lord. One afternoon, several of us boys were hanging around listening to an impromptu lecture on the workings of the human reproductive system, when Tony casually remarked, "By the way, you're gonna burn in hell, you know."

Now I had unquestionably accepted almost all of his pronouncements to date, but here was one that I felt the need to debate.

"Huh?" came my stunning retort (I had a rapier wit in those days). "What was that?"

"You're gonna burn in hell," repeated Tony. "The priest at our church says that if you ain't a Catholic, you ain't goin' to heaven."

"Well, how can I become a Catholic?" I asked, trying not to appear too distraught.

"You can't," said Tony, slowly shaking his head and clasping my shoulder. "You gotta be Italian to be a Catholic."

Great! So because of my nationality, I was destined for the fiery pit. At eleven years of age, I was no stranger to personal tragedy. The Yankees had finished in last place a few seasons ago, and I had spent my vacation in summer school this year. But hell? I was forbidden to use the word, much less spend eternity there! Though it seemed as if I were violating a sacred trust, I felt compelled to verify this information with another source. My circle of friends was somewhat devoid of theologians, so I was going to have to take a chance with this one. I was going to have to ask my dad.

It should be obvious by this point that my religious education left something to be desired. Not that we were heathens, mind you. We were what might be called devout holiday Christians. Never did we miss an Easter or Christmas service—almost never. And Pastor . . . , well his name escapes me, but he was like family.

Anyway, Dad was going to have to field this one, and I spent the next hour getting my nerves together and preparing to use the word *hell* within striking distance of my father's hand. Using the strategy I had initially developed to get test papers signed, I waited until he had the sports section open and calmly walked into his presence.

"Dad, I . . . uh . . . ah . . . well, umm . . . ," I mumbled, as I tried to recall if English was my native language. "Uh . . . Dad, you see . . . ah . . ."

"Have you taken up gargling in the living room, Son, or are you trying to form a sentence?" Dad asked.

And then I just couldn't hold it in any longer. All composure left me, and in that instant—teary-eyed—I blurted out everything that was bothering me. "I don't wanna burn in hell, Dad. I wanna be Italian!"

Whether from the content of my statement or just the accompanying delivery, Dad was caught a little off-guard. He sat there with a look of confusion for a moment, and then— as if a light had come on in his head—he started to grasp the root of my trouble.

"Have you been playing with Anthony, by chance?" Dad asked, his eyebrow beginning to twitch again. "Just what exactly is it that's bothering you?"

For the next hour or so, my father and I talked about God. Not the God I had pictured in my mind, the grandfather type sitting on his throne, but *God*. God, the Creator of the world, the Father of mankind. God, the Son that gave His life on Calvary. God, the One who loved me enough—regardless of my nationality—to sacrifice His only Son, so that I might spend eternity in His presence.

This was not the God that Tony had described. This was *God*. Suddenly, I wanted to know more about Him.

We made a commitment that afternoon as a family to attend church the following Sunday and meet with Pastor what's-his-name. A real understanding didn't come overnight, and many questions surfaced for years to come. If the truth be known, there are questions every day. But we made a beginning that afternoon, thanks to a seed that God planted and to a know-it-all little boy by the name of Tony G.

I have met several "Tony Gs" over the years, but God has given me a more discerning spirit than I possessed as a boy. On occasion, I am forced to stop and evaluate my goals and balance them against what I believe to be God's purpose for my life. Thankfully, one source of knowledge has withstood the test of time. God's Word has never failed to give me the answers I sought, or the comfort I needed.

And by the way, his name was Duncan, Pastor Duncan.

Jesus said,
"Let the little children come to me, and do not hinder them,
for the kingdom of heaven belongs to such as these."
Matthew 19:14

FOUR

A Short-Term Mission from God

For as long as I can remember, a craving to explore the uncharted wilderness filled my waking moments. All I ever wanted to be was a world traveler, and—as is common with twelve-year-old boys—my interests were evidenced in every moment of play and every conversation. A disclaimer is required at this point; this was on Sunday. Had you happened to ask me on Tuesday or Wednesday or Thursday, then all I ever wanted to be was a sea captain, a baseball player, or possibly a hotdog vendor—not necessarily in that order. But as I've pointed out, this was Sunday.

My parents had grown accustomed to my propensity to change career aspirations more frequently than my underwear, and they contented themselves in the knowledge that I was cheap to feed and caused relatively little trouble outside of the home. Not to say that I was maintenance-free, by any means. My recent jaunt into the New York City sewer system (in search of buried treasure) left my parents anxiously anticipating the next change of occupational direction.

"Can't you pretend to be an accountant?" my mother asked as she separated my exploring clothes into baskets marked "bleach" and "burn." "How about a grocer or a teacher or maybe a fireman? Wait! Scratch fireman. I don't even want you to think about becoming a fireman."

"Yeah, Mom. Maybe." Not that I intended to give the idea any serious consideration, but she looked as if she could use the affirmation.

Sitting in the pew that Sunday morning, beneath the vaulted ceilings and stained glass windows, my thoughts returned once again to world travel. Towering above the pulpit stood a visiting missionary. Not at all the meek, quiet man I expected. Probably the result of one-too-many Tarzan movies, I had conjured up a mental picture of a frail little man attached uncomfortably to a heavy wooden pole, destined to serve as kindling for some native fire. But here stood an orator of no small proportion—Johnny Weissmuller with a tie. I listened intently as the missionary addressed our congregation.

He spoke of places straight from the pages of *National Geographic*—great, proud peoples who needed the Word of God, exotic lands and foreign customs, untamed wilds and uncharted territory, powerful tribal chiefs and poor, hungry masses. He spoke, not from a textbook, but from experience. He spoke with authority and conviction. He spoke directly to me.

"And in closing, my Christian brothers and sisters, let me say that our Lord did not call us to spread His Word only where it is convenient, only where it is comfortable, but to spread the Word to all nations, to all people, regardless of their wealth or the color of their skin. I leave you with our Lord's own words: 'Go ye therefore, and teach all nations, baptizing them in the name of the Father, and of the Son, and of the

Holy Ghost.' Will you hear His call, fellow Christians? And more to the point, will you answer it?"

Yes! I wanted to jump to my feet and scream for the entire congregation to hear. Yes, I had heard the call, and yes, I would answer. Filled with enthusiasm, I bolted from the sanctuary before the last note of the closing hymn had drifted to the doorway.

Eager to share this experience with my family, I ran the three blocks that separated the church and our home. With each long stride, I hammered out the particulars of how we would reach our destination. First, we would sell our belongings; that might take a few days. Dad would have to quit his job, but that shouldn't present a problem. Then, there was withdrawing from school; maybe that should be first, in case the folks needed my help. The thought that my family might not fully embrace this venture never occurred to me. After all, God was calling.

Using the wrought-iron railing of our stoop as a brake, I swung myself up the steps and burst through the front door. Chest heaving, lungs gasping for breath, I came to a halt in the living room, prepared to share the news of our good fortune.

"Mom, Dad! We're going to be missionaries!"

"How much is it going to cost?" my father asked from behind the Sunday funnies.

Realizing they failed to grasp the full meaning of the concept, I paused to catch my breath and proceeded with a detailed explanation of our calling and my plan. Thinking it best to save the part about withdrawing from school until the end, I began with the good news about Dad quitting his job.

"Are you crazy?" my father asked.

It became obvious at this point that it might have been necessary for them to actually attend the service in order to hear the call. Hoping to clarify things for them, I recounted the missionary's sermon in full detail and awaited their response.

"Our travel plans for the coming year don't include anything north of the Catskill Mountains or south of the Jersey Shore," my father explained. "If, when you're older, you still want to be a missionary, your mother and I will understand."

Disappointed, but not defeated, I went off to my room to reevaluate the situation. Remembering a piece of Scripture that spoke of a willingness to leave family for the sake of Christ, I reasoned my circumstances as appropriate to the verse and considered my alternatives.

If my parents were unwilling to leave home for the sake of the call, I would have to go it without them. Deeming myself a sort of Christian free agent, I headed to our pastor's residence to offer my services to the visiting missionary.

Following the introductions, the missionary listened to my offer intently, signifying what I assumed to be his agreement with occasional nods of the head. But surprisingly, he agreed with my parents. He talked about God's plan for the family, my need for an education, and something about crossing state lines with a minor. He spoke of the need for missionary supporters right here at home, and how I could be of help through prayer and correspondence. He thanked me for my enthusiasm, but reluctantly declined my offer.

Somewhat older now, I realize that God did call me to the mission field, though not at all as I might have expected. I never made it to Africa or the Far East; I don't speak a foreign language and barely have a command of my own. But He has called me to witness right here, among my friends, neighbors, and coworkers. He has provided for me the resources by which others might travel to far-off lands and allowed me a position of support through prayer and correspondence.

By sharing my testimony and the source of my hope, I am allowed to serve in the way God intended for me. And while

I will never forget that missionary and the sense of disappointment I experienced that day, I smile at the thought of the childish excitement, the willingness to change directions at the drop of a hat. It is with exactly that level of enthusiasm that I hope to meet the Lord's invitations every time He calls.

Then Jesus came to them and said,
"All authority in heaven and on earth has been given to me.
Therefore go and make disciples of all nations,
baptizing them in the name of the Father and of the Son
and of the Holy Spirit, and teaching them to obey everything I
have commanded you. And surely I am with you always, to the
very end of the age."

Matthew 28:18–20

FIVE

Daddy's Little Girl

I don't like to brag, really I don't. But there was a time, not long ago, that I was considered among the world's foremost authorities on every topic known to man. OK, maybe not every topic known to man, but every topic known to little girls—at least, *my* little girl.

Nothing boosts the old ego like having a child hang on your every word, and Melissa hung on mine like cat hair on a dark gray suit. Suddenly I was the Shell Answer Man. Daddy: he knows all, tells all; the man with the plan, the Head Jurassacuda. Daddy can spell all the hard words without looking in the dictionary, understands addition and subtraction, and leaps tall buildings in a single bound.

I loved hearing the words "my daddy says" or "Daddy told me"—the childish equivalent of "No further discussion necessary, thank you very much." If Daddy said it, then that must be the way it is.

But then it happened. We all experience it to one degree or another. Somewhere between "will you walk me to kindergarten?" and "that boy's really cute" the veil is lifted, or possibly torn away, and dads become fallible. Not all at once, as if a major head injury rendered us no longer capable of providing sound advice, but gradually over a brief and painfully disturbing period of time.

I remember the day it happened to me. I was sitting at the breakfast table, fully prepared and ready to dispense vast quantities of fatherly knowledge should the opportunity present itself. Melissa opened the conversation.

"Mr. Braden says that sugar is brain food. It gives us energy and helps get us going in the morning." This she said from behind a bowl of artificial coloring, natural sugar, and milk, her three basic food groups.

I seized the opportunity. "The only thing sugar gets going is your teeth, Melissa," I said, curious as to why someone felt the need to encourage poor eating habits. "Is Mr. Braden thinking of starting a dental practice?"

"I don't know. Maybe," she answered. "There didn't used to be very many dentists, and Mr. Braden said that people used to go to barbers to have their teeth pulled and stuff."

"Well then, maybe Mr. Braden plans to open a salon or possibly a barber shop," I said with more of an edge than my wife felt necessary.

"Time to get dressed and ready for school, kids," Sue said, officially ending our breakfast conversation. Ron and Melissa left the table and headed in the direction of their bedrooms. I immediately noticed a slight chill in the air.

"Was that really necessary?" Sue said.

"Was what really necessary?" I asked. Several years of marriage had taught me to narrow down the question prior to offering the really ignorant answers.

"Your tone of voice," she answered. "Was it really necessary to use that tone of voice? She was just trying to impress you with what she learned."

"Sue, all she learned is an excuse for a morning sugar infusion and not to fall asleep when you're getting your hair done. Who is this guy anyway?"

"If you're referring to Mr. Braden, he's Melissa's second-grade teacher," my wife replied.

"That much I know," I said. "But who is he, really. For crying out loud, the way she talks about him, you'd think he invented the internal combustion engine or found a cure for the common cold. 'Mr. Braden said this,' or 'Mr. Braden said that.' I've got to tell you, Sue, I'm getting awfully tired of hearing Mr. Braden's name around here."

"Has anyone ever told you how cute you look when you're jealous?" Sue said, smiling now that she felt she had gotten to the bottom of things.

"You're being silly," I said. "I don't have a jealous bone in my body. And besides, I don't have anything to be jealous about. I'm just not happy with this guy brainwashing our daughter. I'll tell you something else," I said, on a roll and moving too fast to stop now, "I've had just about enough of the Encyclopedia Braden to last me a lifetime."

Sue was laughing at this point; though she covered her mouth and tried to hide it, she was laughing all the same. "You really are jealous, you know," she said it tenderly, so as not to sound accusing.

"I am not jealous, selfish maybe, but not jealous. I don't know, Sue. Maybe I don't appreciate sharing her attention. I liked it better when Daddy was the voice of authority, not Mr. Braden."

"You better get used to it, Mr. Darbee," Sue said. "It's only going to get worse from now on. She won't stay seven years old forever."

And she didn't; they never do.

Melissa is growing up, and it won't be long before she's ready to leave her mom and dad. There will be another most important man in her life, someone she loves, someone who loves her. That's the way God planned it, even if it's difficult for dads to accept.

There are two other points of consolation in all of this. I will always be the first "most important" man in her life, and Bill Braden won't be the last.

Do not be anxious about anything, but in everything, by prayer and petition, with thanksgiving, present your requests to God. And the peace of God, which transcends all understanding, will guard your hearts and your minds in Christ Jesus.

Philippians 4:6–7

SIX

Stickball Theology

Whoever coined the phrase "you can choose your friends, but you're stuck with your family," didn't grow up in my neighborhood. In New York, friendships were a matter of geography. Imaginary lines—drawn between the deli and the grocery store to the east, the dry cleaner and Arturo's restaurant to the west—had defined the boundaries of our territory from the dawn of time, or at least well beyond my twelve years. As for family, parents bestowed the title of Aunt or Uncle on adults they were particularly fond of. And every woman old enough to handle a wooden spoon was deputized to act as your mother.

Leaving the security of this extended family to seek friendships in other parts of the city was not unheard of—nor were the consequences. More than one daring young man had ventured beyond Arturo's to return victimized by boys none too happy with a stranger in their midst. Not that this was life-threatening. There were no guns or knives to contend with in those days. Gang violence was a marking of your territory, and embarrassment was the tool. A wandering socialite might return minus his sneakers, which could be seen hanging—in trophy fashion—from a third-story clothesline several blocks away. Having the waistband of your underwear yanked up around the vicinity of your ears was another sign of welcome common to our area, one that I intended to avoid.

Our circle of friends functioned with this sense of community. Living in the neighborhood meant acceptance to the group—a caste system of sorts, based on apartment number or street address. Not to say that we didn't quarrel or disagree; we argued all the time—about important things, like could the Dodgers be considered a New York team even though they had moved to Los Angeles? (A move, we were sure, that the players had fought tooth and nail.) We debated the roles of Italians, Irishmen, and Jews in determining the events of history. Religion was also a frequent point of discussion, not because of any strong theological convictions, but because we were each raised to accept that our own system of beliefs was the only path to salvation, and to consider anything else was sin.

I remember one conversation on a warm Sunday afternoon, the weather just right for stickball. (The weather was always right for stickball, at least until somebody's mother announced otherwise.) A group of boys was sitting on the steps of our home, waiting for the team captains to choose sides. Elliot Pelzman and Tony Gianelli were always the captains—Elliot, because he was the best player; Tony, because he had the biggest mouth. The process of picking sides was not of great interest to me, as I was what was known as a "you get."

"You get Darbee," Tony said, after the others were chosen.

As I took my place behind Elliot, Tony—with all the tact of a practiced statesman—introduced our topic of discussion.

"So, Darb," Tony chided. "What did you do in church today? You learn how to turn bread into wine yet?"

"Don't you mean water into wine?" Elliot questioned, coming to my defense.

"What do you know?" Tony asked. "You're Jewish, for Pete's sake!"

"I know the difference between bread and water," Elliot said.

If anyone questioned his infallibility, Tony would usually let loose with a barrage of verbal assaults. However, Elliot was granted special dispensation from this treatment, "out of respect," Tony claimed, though I suspected the fact that Elliot was a full head taller may have lent to Tony's sense of benevolence.

"So, what did you learn, anyway?" Tony asked, attempting to regain control of the conversation.

"The pastor told us we should try to be more accum . . . ecumu . . . ecumenical," I said, stumbling over the five-dollar word.

"What's ecumenical?" one boy asked.

"Ecumenicals are the white parts around your fingernails," responded Mickey, the youngest of our group.

"Those are cuticles, Einstein!" Tony said, still trying to redeem himself. "Don't you know anything?"

"So what does ecumenical mean, Tony?" Elliot asked, anxious to see Tony squirm.

"What am I, a dictionary?" Tony said. "I'm not gonna be around forever to answer your questions! You tell 'em, Darbee."

"Well . . . ," I started, fully aware that I was setting myself up for the kill. "I think it has something to do with all Christians worshiping together."

"They'd need a pretty big building," Mickey said.

"I don't think Pastor Duncan meant everyone worshiping in one building, Mickey," I said. "I think it's more of an attitude. The way we treat Christians from different churches, or something."

"We're already ecumenical," Tony said. "Didn't St. Mary's lend your church the Knights of Columbus hall to have your dinner last month?"

"Yeah," I conceded. "But I think it's more than that."

"Well, if you mean being allowed to marry my sister," Tony countered, "you'd better think again. She's gonna marry a Catholic."

The thought of being considered an ineligible suitor for Tony's sister was not a major disappointment in my life. I knew Mary Gianelli. She would wrestle you to the ground if she felt you had wronged her in some way. Mary could spit farther—and more often—than any boy on the block. One or two of the Catholic boys looked as if they were considering changing denominations based on this information alone.

"Nobody wants to marry your sister, Tony," I said.

"You better not let her hear you say that," warned Elliot.

"What I mean is, I think it's more like not looking at other churches in terms of 'Us and Them,'" I said. "I guess I don't understand it either."

As usual, the conversation ended as quickly as it started—stickball being less confusing than theology. Yet I couldn't help but wonder about the pastor's sermon and how it must have pertained to us in some way. Early the next morning, I went to the church office and—after giving Pastor Duncan the details of the previous day's conversation—asked him to explain.

"For starters," Pastor began, "you don't have to marry Anthony's sister. The point I was trying to make is that when we invite Christ into our lives and welcome Him as Savior, we become one small but important part of a greater body. In essence, we become one 'body' in Christ. Now, while some may choose to worship in settings that are more formal or traditional, others seek to express their love for God in different ways. It is not so important how we worship, as long as we are worshiping the one true God and doing so in a way that will glorify Him. Do you understand?"

"I think so," I said. "Does this mean that everyone who goes to church will go to heaven?"

"No, that's not what I meant," the pastor continued. "There are no magic portals in sanctuary doors that will allow you to pass into heaven. Many people associate themselves with a particular church or denomination but still lack a real relationship with God. It is through Christ that we have been saved, and it is that relationship that makes us one body. Is that any better?"

"Yeah, I understand," I said. "Sorry to take up all your time."

"It's no bother at all," Pastor assured me. "Would you like me to visit and explain this to your friends?"

"No, but thanks anyway," I replied. "I wouldn't want you to get your underwear pulled up around your ears."

"I appreciate that!" Pastor said. "If you ever have any questions, my door is open."

"Thanks, Pastor Duncan. I think I'm OK for now."

Looking back, I see a group of boys who understood ecumenism better than they thought. While certain criteria existed to set us apart from everyone else, there was an air of acceptance—an agreement to be free to disagree.

Over the years, God has given me the opportunity to worship in diverse settings, with people from a myriad of backgrounds and personal preferences. I have seen God praised beneath the light of stained glass windows and among the trees of the forest, in crowded cities and suburban neighborhoods, in great halls and rented rooms. When these differences leave me wondering about the unity of the body of Christ, I remember the first ecumenical thinker. One who brought together fishermen and a tax collector. One who ate with Pharisees and prostitutes. One who gave me the gift of life.

Just as each of us has one body with many members,
and these members do not all have the same function,
so in Christ we who are many form one body,
and each member belongs to all the others.

Romans 12:4–5

SEVEN

The Great Male Bonding Weekend

He jumps! He shoots! He scores!" I screamed as the miniature sponge basketball sank through the net hanging from the living room door. A few victory laps around the coffee table, index fingers extended, and a chant of "I'm number one! I'm number one!" provoked my son into an unflattering bout of poor sportsmanship. (Where do kids pick up this stuff?)

"You cheat!" he yelled.

I took a quick glance over each shoulder, convinced he was addressing someone else.

"You cheat!" he repeated.

"I'm sorry. Were you talking to me? I know you weren't talking to me," I said, "because if you were, you would have addressed me with respect. You would have called me by a name suitable for someone of my advanced athletic stature. Something like 'Champ' or 'Hoopster,' maybe even 'Grand Master of Roundball.'" I felt another victory lap coming on.

"You shoved me and your hand was in my face! You can't do that!"

"I out-played you, Son. I simply applied a little pressure under the net, and you folded. It's called technique."

"It's called cheating."

"Hey, you say tomato . . ." I paused for effect. "I'll tell you what. We'll make it best-out-of-three, but then Jake takes the winner." Jake was on the couch, laughing hysterically or suffering from some sort of violent convulsions. Either way, the boy obviously wasn't used to witnessing healthy communication.

"Is your dad always like this?" Jake asked.

"Only when we miss a dose of his medication," Ron answered. "By the way, don't leave anything sharp lying around."

This was day two of our "bachelor weekend." The women in our lives had abandoned us in favor of a mother/daughter retreat. Since Jake's mom was a single parent, he joined Ron and me to complete our "Three Musketeers." Actually, had his mother believed for a moment that Jake would eat anything *besides* Three Musketeers, he might have stayed home alone. But as it turned out, he stayed with us. We were glad to have him, and we needed the referee.

"You know, I've worked up quite a thirst with all this celebrating," I said. "What say we hit the kitchen and grab some refreshments." Two teenagers bolting from the room produced a refreshing breeze, and I followed along in their draft.

"I'll get the milk," my son said.

"I'll get the glasses," Jake offered.

"Stop, hold it right there," I said. "Boys, you obviously don't understand the finer points of a bachelor weekend. Allow me to explain. Rule number one: Toilet seats are to remain in the raised position. Rule number two: There is no distinction between hand towels and dish towels. And number three: No glasses. We drink out of the cartons."

"How come?" Ron asked.

"Because we can. Now each of you mark a carton with your name. I don't want your nasty little lips on my milk carton."

Sprawled across the living room floor, drinking from our individual cartons, we passed the time with a little conversation. The subjects of sports, cars, and, of course, sports cars having been exhausted the day before, the boys chose to educate me on a proper masculine image.

"Nothing personal, Mr. Darbee," Jake said, "but don't you think this whole bachelor weekend thing is kinda lame?"

"Define lame," I said.

"Well, you know, like weak, senseless."

"I'm not following you."

"What he means, Dad," my son joined in, "is if you're the man of the house, why do we need all these rules for a bachelor weekend? You're in charge, right? Why can't we do all this stuff when Mom's around?"

"I get it," I said. "What you're trying to say is I'm the king of the castle, lord of the manor, that sort of thing."

"Right," Jake said.

"Things will be different when I'm married," Ron said. "If I want to drink from the carton or eat with my hands, I will. Nobody's gonna tell me what to do. Besides, it's biblical."

"Biblical?" I questioned. "Please, share with me the source of your scholarly knowledge."

"It's Ephesians 5:22," Jake said. "We read it in Sunday School last week. 'Wives, submit to your husbands as to the Lord.'"

"I see. And this you chose to memorize. I mean with all the Scripture at your fingertips, this is the verse that spoke to your hearts?"

"Yeah," they responded.

"OK. I think I understand the problem," I said, pick–ing up a Bible to use as a visual aid. "This is the Word of God, gentlemen, not a fortune cookie. You cannot read one verse and apply it at your convenience. Read verse twenty-five."

Ron took the Bible and turned to Ephesians 5. "Husbands, love your wives, just as Christ loved the church and gave himself up for her," he read.

"And would that indicate, then, that some personal sacrifice might be necessary on your part?" I said.

"Can we get back to you?" Jake asked. The boys left the room to reevaluate their position.

Late that afternoon, the women returned home, signifying an end to our bachelor weekend. Always the perfect gentleman, I held the door as the ladies carried in their luggage.

"Mom, there are three open milk cartons in the refrigerator, and they all have lip prints on them," my daughter announced, inspecting the contents for any other signs of violation.

"I can explain that, Dear," I told my wife.

"Well you know how I love a good story," my wife said, "but wait just a minute and I'll be back. It was a long trip."

As my wife left the room, our son suddenly remembered a problem. "Oh yeah, Dad. The light's out in the bathroom. I think it needs—"

"Eeeeeyaaah" *Splash!* The scream cut him off in mid sentence.

"What do you say we head over to the school and shoot some hoops?" I said. "Or would you boys care to share that memory verse with your mothers?" Ron rushed to find the basketball. Jake had kissed his mother and was already out the door.

"Melissa, hand this to Mom, and tell her we'll see her later. And welcome home, Sweetheart."

"But this is a dish towel," she said.

"That's OK. It's an emergency."

In this same way,
husbands ought to love their wives as their own bodies.
He who loves his wife loves himself.

Ephesians 5:28

EIGHT

Work of My Hands

Is that a Pinewood Derby kit I see in your hand?" I asked. Ron was eight years old at the time and returning home from a Boy's Brigade meeting at our church. He held the box up high as he came into the living room, extended out for me to see. There was no mistaking the rectangular block of pine, the black plastic wheels, the familiar decals. It was Pinewood Derby time all right.

"Mr. Acaya said we're supposed to work on these with our fathers," Ron said. "Will you help me build mine, Dad?"

I thought he'd never ask. "Are you kidding? Just try and stop me. Hey, did I ever tell you your grandfather and I built a few of these when I was your age?" His eyes opened a little wider as he shook his head from side to side. "We won best looking car two years in a row," I continued. "I'll bet the trophies are still in Grandma's basement somewhere."

"Cool."

"You bet it's cool," I said. "Now listen, pal, this is important." I got down on one knee to address him at eye level. "Anyone can build a Pinewood Derby car, but it takes a lot of effort to produce a winner." I had his full attention.

"I need to know, are you willing to put forth the effort?" I held up one hand to indicate there was more to come before he'd be required to answer. "It'll mean giving up some playtime and television shows to work on your car; it won't always seem like fun." I paused for dramatic effect. "Son," I said, back on my feet and placing a hand on each of his shoulders, "do you have what it takes to be a winner?"

"I guess."

"Good enough," I said. "We'll start tomorrow as soon as I get home from work. Now go get ready for bed."

"Honey," I said, turning toward my wife. "I'm telling you, I can smell the wood glue already. Sawdust in our eyes, the taste of spray paint blowing back in our faces—this is going to be a true father/son bonding experience."

"How much of that glue did you say you smelled already?" she asked.

"Very funny, Miss Cynical, but I'm telling you, this is going to be an unforgettable experience for Ron, something he'll remember for the rest of his life."

"Like the time you lost your eyebrows lighting the barbecue grill?"

"*One* eyebrow," I said, "and you can laugh if you want to, but he's going to love it. You wait and see. This car is going to turn out great."

"Just promise me you'll be careful out there," she said. "And supervise him around the power tools. I'm going to count fingers every night at dinner, and if he's missing anything, you'd better be prepared to donate."

Excited about the prospect of working on this project with my son, I could hardly contain myself. I stopped by the local hardware store on my way home from work the next evening and picked up a few necessities.

"That should just about do it," I said, talking to myself as I made a final scan of the pegboard lining the aisle. "Jigsaw blades, there we go. Can't forget the saw blades." I carried my basket of purchases to a young man at the first available register.

"Let me guess," he said, running my merchandise over the scanner. "Wood putty, six grades of sandpaper, glue, spray paint. It's Pinewood Derby time, right?"

"How did you guess?"

"After the first six or seven fathers, a guy catches on. Say, did you forget the graphite? All the other fathers bought graphite to lubricate the wheels."

I bought the graphite and thanked the cashier for his assistance before attempting to set a new land speed record on my drive home. *I can't believe I almost forgot the graphite. What was I thinking? So the competition got there ahead of us. Must have taken a day off from work,* I thought. *Probably a bunch of those domineering, overbearing father types you always hear about. Well, I just hope they don't ruin it for the kids.*

Ron and I rushed through dinner, anxious to get down to the business at hand.

"First, we need a design," I told my son. "Something unique, yet streamlined enough to hold its own in the time trials. We're shooting for 'Best Looking,' but we have to make a decent showing for speed or it won't mean anything. Got any ideas?"

"I kinda thought we could make it like this," the novice said as he grabbed the pine block from my hand and started scratching lines with my carpenter's pencil.

"Hey, what do you think you're doing?" I asked, retrieving the block and pencil and erasing the newly drawn lines. "Never, ever draw on the wood, Son. That's the first rule of craftsmanship. First you sketch out the design on paper, then you lightly trace it onto the wood. Pay attention now and you might learn something."

"Now what do you think," I said, "stock car, drag racer, or midget? What will it be?"

"I want it to look like this." He reached for the pencil again, but I cut him off before he could do any damage.

"I'll tell you what, Ron," I said. "This is a real tough part of the project. Why don't you let me handle the design, and we'll save you for the actual building. Think of it like sitting in the bullpen ready to save the game. How does that sound?"

"OK, I guess." He took a seat at my workbench and watched intently as I sketched out our design. Three pencils and most of a drafting pad later, the design was good enough to transfer from paper.

"Now we're ready to make the cuts," I announced, pulling my jigsaw from its spot in the rafters. "What do you say to that?"

"Cool," Ron answered. "Can I cut it out, Dad? Can I?"

"You know what, Ron," I said. "I think Dad's gonna do the actual cutting, but you get to put the wood in the vise. Here you go, son. Not too tight now, you don't want to dent it. Here, maybe you better let me do that." I finished setting the block in the vise and began making the initial cuts. A few minutes later our basic design was starting to take shape.

"Ready to try your hand at sanding, Ron?" I asked. He appeared lost in his own little world, sitting at the workbench making designs in the sawdust with a screwdriver. (The kid didn't have much of an attention span.)

"Sure, Dad." I handed him a section of medium-grade paper and instructed him in the fine art of sanding. He started out strong but veered off course in a matter of minutes.

"Ron, you have to go with the grain," I corrected, taking the block from his hand. "Let me show you what I mean."

Thirty minutes of sanding with increasingly finer papers provided a smooth surface for our first coat of paint—sealer actually, to keep the wood from soaking up the paint. "OK, Ron," I said. "Climb onto the mound and start warming up . . . Hey, Ron! Ron, where did you go?"

As we prepared for bed that evening, I mentioned to my wife my disappointment with Ron's lack of motivation toward our project. "I just don't understand it, Sue. You'd think he'd enjoy working on something with his dad."

"Yes, it is difficult to understand," she said. "What part didn't he seem to enjoy?"

"I don't know. I thought he enjoyed it all just fine."

"Well, how much of it did you let him do by himself?"

"Come on, Sue," I said. "It's his project. I let him do all of it, pretty much. Of course I gave him a hand here and there, but for the most part, he did all the work."

Her look indicated a smidgen of doubt, so I thought it best to provide specific examples in support of my case. "The design was all his, mostly, except for the drawing and the tracing part and stuff," I said. "Oh, you know what? The cutting, he really liked the cutting part, so I let him put the wood in the vise . . . sort of. Sanding! I let him do some sanding . . ." Reality started to sink in. "Oh boy," I said, sitting down on the bed. "Did I blow it. Sue, I've turned into my dad."

Breakfast the next morning found me apologizing and trying to explain the previous night's actions to my son. "Ron, I'm awfully sorry, pal. I don't know what got into me. It's your project, son, and I pushed you right out of it. I am sorry."

"That's OK, Dad."

"I appreciate you saying that, Ron," I said, "but it's not OK, not really. I guess there are a few things we fathers pass down from generation to generation, and apparently this is one of them. Your grandfather did the same thing to me when

I was a Cub Scout, and from what I hear, so did his father before him."

"Does this mean we get to make another one?" Ron asked, a hint of interest in his voice again.

"Sure thing, Ron. We'll make any kind of car you like," I said. "And here," I handed him a piece of scrap pine I had in the garage that was roughly the same dimensions as his kit. "We can start with this."

"I know exactly what I want to make," he said and started drawing lines on the block.

"Now hold on just a minute, pal," I said. "Always draw on—"

"Step away from the wood," my wife's voice called from behind hands cupped in a makeshift megaphone. "You in the business suit, raise your hands above your head and step away from the wood."

"You know what, Ron," I said. "I think you're right. Go ahead and draw however you like."

When I was a boy in my father's house, still tender,
and an only child of my mother, he taught me and said,
"Lay hold of my words with all your heart;
keep my commands and you will live."

Proverbs 4:3–4

NINE

'Tis the Season

Dad! Dad!" my son yelled as he burst into the den, interrupting the solitude of my quiet time.

"What is it, and how much will it cost?" I asked, assuming his urgency was financially motivated.

"Nothing, Dad. It's not always about money, you know."

"Sorry, Son. What's so important?"

"You know that father/son bonding stuff you're always talking about? Well, Mom is going nuts, and now would be a great time."

"What did you do?" I asked, concerned that his sudden desire to bond with the old man might somehow stem from a bent for self-preservation.

"Nothing! I mean it."

"Then what did I do?" (It never hurts to check.)

"I don't think you did anything, either," he said. "It's Mom. She was baking Christmas cookies and just started acting crazy. Now she's crying because she can't get the top off the Midol bottle."

"Ohhhh," I said, the situation suddenly clear. "We have what is called a crisis situation, my boy. Conditions require that we make ourselves scarce."

"What about Melissa?" he asked, referring to his little sister.

"She's down the block playing with Sarah," I said. "And besides, they never go after one of their own. It's you and me I'm worried about. Where is your mother now?"

"In the garage. She's tearing up your workbench looking for that 'cutting thing.' I think she means the scroll saw."

A chill ran up my spine at the mention of power tools. "Honey, wait!" I yelled through the walls. "Don't plug anything in. I'll be right there." I turned to my son to relay the game plan. "OK. I'm going in. If you don't hear from me in ten minutes, come and get me."

"No way."

"Chicken," I said, going for the soft underbelly of adolescent pride. "And after all the tight spots I've pulled you out of."

"Don't think I don't appreciate it, Dad. Good luck getting the cap off that bottle." He patted me on the back and sent me on my way.

Times arise in every man's life when he must stare directly into the face of danger and confront it. Thankfully, I got that out of my system while serving with the Marines. I opened the door to the garage. "Honey," I said, "can I help you with anything?"

"You can try to take the top off of this bottle, or show me how to start the chain saw," Sue said.

Following the manufacturer's instructions, I pushed down while turning and presented my wife with the open bottle. I chose not to flaunt my success at that particular moment and exited post-haste.

Moments later, I returned to the den and found my son deeply engrossed in a game of Nintendo. "Mission completed," I informed him. I pointed to the television screen. "I can tell you were worried about me."

"I knew you could handle it, Dad." He put the game on pause. "Hey, Dad? Why is it Mom always gets like this around the holidays? She really seems to freak out around Christmas."

"Tradition," I said.

"Tradition?"

"Yeah, you know: stringing popcorn and cranberries, carols around the tree, anxiety attack—happens every year. Your grandmother used to get spun up, and her mother before her. It's tradition."

"How come?"

"Mom works hard to make sure everything is just right at Christmas, Ron," I said. "If she gets a little anxious, we can give her some room."

"I know, but you guys are always saying that all that stuff doesn't matter. Jesus is supposed to be the focus, right? Why does Mom get so worried about the details?"

"I guess she wants everything to be perfect," I said. "You and I both know she understands the real meaning of Christmas. In her own way, Mom is performing an act of service. By sweating all the details, I think she figures it'll be easier for the rest of us to celebrate and enjoy Christ's presence."

"So what do we do?" he asked.

"Nothing," I said. "We sit here and hide in the den like real men."

Grabbing the other controller, I sat on the floor and joined him in his game: Mario and Luigi attempting to avoid the mighty Koopa. One couldn't help but notice the irony.

An hour or so passed and things were looking up for Mario and Luigi. We quit our game and listened for sounds of life outside our sanctuary. All was quiet, no sign of life, save the smell of freshly baked cookies. It was too much for my son, as weak-willed as most boys when matters of the stomach are involved.

"Dad, do you smell those cookies?" he asked, his eyes as big as saucers, a hint of saliva at the edge of his lips.

"No, I do not," I said, squeezing my nose between thumb and index finger. "If you know what's good for you, you don't smell them either."

"Come on, Dad. I can be in and out of there before anyone knows it. I'll just grab a couple."

"I want to go on record as saying this is a mistake," I lectured. "But if you are determined to follow this course of action, so be it. Don't forget the milk."

Following at a distance, I monitored his progress. My boy edged his way out of the den, through the hallway, and into the kitchen. Deep down, I was rooting for him, though I doubted the probability of a triumphant return. For a moment, it appeared he might succeed.

"Get your hands away from those cookies!" screeched a familiar feminine voice. "Don't you even think about eating them. Those are for Christmas." Ron made a hasty retreat back to the safety of the den.

"You forgot the milk."

"Sorry, Dad. I don't know how it slipped my mind. So what do we do now?" he asked, looking to his mentor for direction. "The cookies are out of the question, and I don't think we want to push Mom right now."

"We could wrap presents," I suggested. "Just the two of us. It might be kind of nice."

"I haven't done any shopping yet, Dad. We've still got a week."

"Yeah, me either. Well, we could go outside and hang the lights. That'll kill an hour."

"You're not going to put the lights up with a staple gun again this year, are you?" he asked. "I'd hate to think electrocution is going to be another family tradition."

"No, I bought these little hooks that were made for the job," I said. "You go bring the ladder out front and I'll pull the lights down from the attic. Oh, and Son, have a cookie. I palmed a couple while your mother was yelling at you. Merry Christmas."

"Thanks, Dad. Merry Christmas to you, too."

"So do not worry, saying, 'What shall we eat?' or
'What shall we drink?' or 'What shall we wear?'
For the pagans run after all these things,
and your heavenly Father knows that you need them.
But seek first his kingdom and his righteousness,
and all these things will be given to you as well.
Therefore do not worry about tomorrow,
for tomorrow will worry about itself.
Each day has enough trouble of its own."

Matthew 6:31–34

Wanted: Dad

And now we will attempt to reattach the leg," I said. The room was thick with tension, all eyes focused on my steady, capable hands and the slender, young blonde woman lying prostrate on the table before me. Though I had performed this intricate surgical procedure at least a dozen times, each situation was unique and fraught with its own unique complications.

The bright overhead lights reflected from the glistening bead of perspiration forming on my brow as I prepared to forge ahead. Running one last time through the mental checklist, I shot a final glance at the instrument tray, surveying the essential equipment. Satisfied with the level of preparation, I raised my head and intercepted a nod of confidence from my assisting surgeon.

"Pliers," I said, extending my hand in the direction of my assistant. Eyes closed, squeezing for all I was worth, I listened for the sound that would identify success or failure. *SNAP!*

Opening only one eye at first, and finally the other, I looked down—hoping for the best, but prepared for the worst. I exhaled a sigh of relief.

"It appears Barbie will regain complete use of her leg, Melissa," I said to my daughter. Setting down the pliers, I leaned back in the kitchen chair, stretched, and waited for the sounds of accolades to fill the room.

"Thanks, Dad." *Snatch, whooshhhh* . . . gone.

Alone, Barbie-less, and with enough tools to assemble a small nuclear reactor, I was left to contemplate the meaning of life, or maybe fatherhood, or maybe how I could get the mess cleaned up before Sue got home. No such luck.

"Hello, Dear. Did you have a nice afternoon?" I asked. Sue has always shown a remarkable appreciation for tools and today was no exception. So overwhelmed was she by the enormous display scattered about the kitchen, several moments passed before she could manage a sentence.

"I thought we agreed not to rebuild engines in the kitchen," she said.

"We did. I was just putting the leg back on Melissa's Barbie doll."

"So why the entire Craftsman line?" Sue asked. "A simple pair of pliers would suffice."

A lucky guess if you ask me. But then again, the woman does know her hand tools.

Doll repair is, of course, just one of the tasks at which I have gained proficiency over the course of my fathering tenure. I don't remember "minor surgery" appearing in the job description when I agreed to accept this position. Come to think of it, I don't remember receiving any job description at all.

Maybe that's what fathers need, a job description, something that lists the qualifications for our position and the recommended experience levels. At least that way, we would know what's expected. We would have a measuring stick, something to compare ourselves to during those times we felt like we fell short of the mark. It would probably read something like this:

Wanted—Dad

Start-up family seeks male role model to assume leadership position in a small, growing concern.

Nature and Scope of Position: Potential mother seeks father figure to assist with the twenty-four-hour, seven-day-per-week operation of a dedicated family unit. This position entails working in close partnership with one female counterpart, diametrically opposed in physical makeup and emotional character, with a strong possibility of conflicting parental philosophies. Must prove capable of achieving consensus on most issues and appearing united when presenting information to subordinates. This is a long-term position, offering tremendous growth potential, and permanent employment status. Termination prior to fulfilling all contractual obligations will result in strict penalties due to the damage caused the corporate body.

Essential Duties: Generate sufficient income, either alone or in conjunction with female partner, to support the needs of the family unit. Provide spiritual, physical, and emotional support to all team members, with special emphasis on raising, training, and protecting children, newborn to undetermined ages. Assist in the integration of change and the resolution of problems brought about by difficult circumstances and seemingly impossible challenges that threaten personal enjoyment and comfort levels. Various other duties include, but are not limited to: changing diapers, burying expired pets, repairing bicycle

tires, monitoring homework, modeling appropriate behavior, and occasionally dispensing discipline. This list is
by no means complete. For a comprehensive listing of essential duties see: Grandfather.

Attributes/Skills Required/Sought: Must be honest,
conscientious, and hard-working. Patience, dedication,
and loyalty a definite plus. Demonstrated ability to attempt plumbing, carpentry, mechanical and electrical
tasks, regardless of actual ability, a must.

Experience/Education Required/Sought: No experience
necessary; training provided on the job. Entry-level position open to men of varying ages without regard to race or
national origin. No education required, but minimum of
high school diploma strongly preferred.

Salary Information: Salary and benefits commensurate
with "Mom" position. No direct financial compensation
available, however, many intangible gains in the form of
love, respect, and admiration. (Disclosure: these are examples of typical intangible gains. The intangible gains
you receive may be similar or different depending on the
individual situation. Intangible gains may appear nonex-
istent during junior team members' adolescent years.)

Admittedly, the experienced father may notice a few glar-
ing omissions and wonder if he has somehow assumed duties
not normally associated with his position. Fear not, such is the
way with job descriptions. They provide candidates with
enough information to screen out the unqualified, but not so
much as to scare away the really hot prospects.

In fairness, a complete and accurate job description,
something exhaustive enough to provide a reasonable and
honest representation of all paternal duties, would require vol-
umes rivaling Britannica and rank for sheer horror at par with

the collected works of Stephen King. Prospective applicants, overwhelmed with the scope of the job and stricken with fear, would begin throwing themselves off bridges, behavior not normally associated with fathering for at least the first thirteen years.

Necessary omissions would include anything related to "some adult assembly required," questions such as "where do babies come from," and the entire chapter discussing a father's interaction with his in-laws. Just to be safe, it might be best to avoid a detailed description of Dad's duties in teaching the kids to drive or explaining to insurance agents the irony in junior's perception of the federal speed limit laws.

Maybe it is better that we don't have a detailed job description after all. Is knowing about all the negative possibilities worth the risk of missing out on the entire "dad" experience? I don't think so. Perhaps we could use a job description that gave us all the pertinent information, but left a little to the imagination. Possibly something like this:

Wanted—Dad

Must love God with all his heart, with all his soul, and with all his strength and be willing to share that love with a child. All other skills trainable.

Yup, I think that sums it up rather nicely.

Train a child in the way he should go,
and when he is old he will not turn from it.

Proverbs 22:6

ELEVEN

Growing Pains

I don't mind the idea of my children growing up, really I don't. In fact, there are times when I relish the thought, dream about it, contemplate it with great expectation. Not many times, mind you, but a few; usually on days spent untangling an angry cat from thirty feet of mini-blind cord or filling in the backyard tunnel that fell a few feet short of China. Still, most of the time I enjoy watching them grow, seeing the changes take place as their characters develop. Sometimes though, I'd like a little more warning.

My wife recently brought news of the latest development in our daughter's life.

"You'll never guess what I'm going to pick up at the store," my wife said snatching the car keys and heading for the door. Years of marriage had taught me that while the question seemed rhetorical on the surface, a token guess was obligatory.

"Twinkies," I answered. Twinkies were a neutral, middle-of-the-road sort of guess that couldn't possibly elicit any accusations of insensitivity.

"No, silly. A training bra."

"I think I'd rather have the Twinkies."

"Well, we don't need Twinkies," my wife said. "We need a training bra."

Again, I thought carefully before responding. This half of "we" certainly wasn't in the market for a training bra, even if I had let myself go a bit. Since I grew up without the benefit of sisters, I decided to follow up with a typically thoughtless line of questioning.

"A training bra?" I asked, not yet grasping the obvious. "Why do you need a training bra?" The sudden change in her expression signaled that I was not doing well in this conversation.

"It's not for me, smart aleck. It's for our daughter."

"Our daughter!" sure that I had misheard her somehow. "Did you say *our daughter?*"

"Yes, our daughter. You remember, brown hair, blue eyes, lives down the hall in the second room on the left."

"But she can't need a training bra; she's not old enough."

"Not old enough," my wife said. "Do you have a chart that tells you when she's old enough?"

"No," I answered, "but I've been thinking about making one up. You know, that really isn't a bad idea. If we surveyed enough parents, I'm sure we could come up with—

"She needs a bra."

"Now wait a minute," I argued. "She's just a little girl. I bet she'd rather have one of those cute Barney T-shirts or something with Barbie on the back."

"I'm going to arrange counseling for you."

"What if we bought her some baggy sweaters or something? You know, the extra-large look is pretty popular. She likes wool, maybe burlap even."

"I'm dialing the pastor now."

"Wait. Don't you understand? She's just not ready. I'm not ready. If we buy her a bra, it's like admitting she's growing up. Boys will start to look at her differently. She'll start dating, fall in love, get married. What if she moves to New Jersey? We'll never see our grandchildren!"

My wife walked into the kitchen and returned with a brown paper lunch bag. "Breathe into this," she said, "and listen. We're talking about a perfectly normal child experiencing a perfectly normal stage of development. To the best of my knowledge she has not, as of yet, chosen a china pattern or registered at the bridal boutique. Now, as her perfectly normal mother and her . . . ah . . . father, I think we need to relax and be supportive."

"So you really think she needs this thing?" I asked. "We're not rushing her?"

"She asked me to buy it. I think that's our best indication."

Acceptance started to set in at this point as I remembered that growing up was part of God's plan. Melissa would continue to change and become more independent, whether I chose to accept it or not. Besides, this hurdle was almost behind us now and, in time might not seem like such a big deal.

"You're absolutely right, Dear. I don't know why I made such a fuss. I'll see you when you get back from the mall."

"Can I get you anything while I'm out?" Sue asked.

The phone rang in the next room before I had a chance to answer. A moment later my daughter's voice called in question. "Can Alan come over and do homework with me?" she asked.

"Come to think of it, there are a few things I could use," I said, ignoring Melissa's question. "Thirty yards of barbed wire, an alarm system, and a case of dog food."

"We don't have a dog," my wife said.

"Oh yeah, and a dog. A big dog."

"Therefore do not worry about tomorrow, for tomorrow will worry about itself. Each day has enough trouble of its own."

Matthew 6:34

I Am PEST,
Hear Me Roar!

It seems like only yesterday that Ron sought me out for life's difficult questions, like, "Daddy, where do hamsters go after you flush?" and "Did Grandma really fly here on a broom?"

Then it happened—a massive infusion of hormones surged through Ron's cranium and ravaged his young body. Vital sections of a once functioning brain were impaired, adversely affecting his hearing ("You didn't tell me to take out the garbage"), memory ("I don't remember you telling me to take out the garbage"), and motor skills ("I was going to take out the garbage, but I couldn't get the lid off the can").

Thankfully the damage appears limited to chores and other areas important only to a parent, leaving the victim free to enjoy loud music, hours of Nintendo, and an active social life.

I'm thinking about starting a support group for other parents of teenagers. It would be a place where moms and dads get together for an hour or so each week to discuss some of the more troubling aspects of adolescence. We would limit ourselves to deep, heartfelt conversations on the psychological trauma being visited upon our children and waste no time griping or complaining about its effects on us. We would call our group: "PEST — Parents Enthusiastically Serving Teenagers."

I have already collected several possible topics for our discussions, any one of which could conceivably carry the group through the entire adolescent period. For example:

Independence—My son has a unique definition of independence that includes making all of his own decisions, such as: what to eat, where to go, and when to come home. As a father, I need not trouble myself with the petty details of his life. My role is one of support, providing the means for him to live, as in: food, clothing, and shelter. Oh yeah, and money. I'm supposed to provide the money.

So far, we're still trying to define the middle ground in our house. Hopefully, we'll reach consensus somewhere between indentured servant (his definition) and human sponge (go ahead, guess).

Diet—Scientific evidence supports the belief that your average teenager can survive, dare I say thrive, on a diet that would kill an otherwise healthy lab rat in two weeks. Most adolescents believe that food preparation consists of a paper sack passing through the car window and money exchanging hands. Washing down a hamburger with a six-pack of cola ranks among the top ten seven-course meals, followed closely by three cans of chili, two Twinkies, and a pair of two-liter sodas.

If for some reason—like say brain damage—you or I attempted to sustain life for an extended period of time on the standard teenage eating plan, we would surely require extensive medical attention. On a recent camping trip, I made the mistake of putting my son in charge of food supplies. I suffered a gastroenterological phenomenon previously experienced by only a handful of careless fire-eating acts and possibly a few White House Press Secretaries.

Rest—Eight hours of sleep is pretty much standard for the adult world, but not so in the land of adolescence. In complete contrast to what a parent might normally presume, a teenager requires remarkably little sleep during the school week. Much of the needed weekday rest comes during periods of near comatose meditation called "class." Chemistry, physics, and psychology lend themselves to a mild form of suspended consciousness while forty-five minutes of trigonometry leaves teachers checking for organ donor cards.

Weekends, of course, are an entirely different subject. To expect a youth to rise before noon is ludicrous; to require such awkward behavior borders on cruel and unusual punishment. Just who suffers the punishment remains a topic of some heated debate.

Schedules—Getting up every morning and commuting an hour to work struck me as quite a drudgery until I took a day off and watched my wife try to get the kids out of the house on time. Now I nearly skip to the car, whistling a happy tune every bouncy step of the way. PEST groups will find countless hours of discussion material when they broach the subject of schedules.

So much do I dislike trying to rush our kids along, I volunteered to usher at the morning services each Sunday as an excuse to leave the house early and drive a separate car. Sue doesn't mind in the least; she likes being seated by someone who doesn't give her dirty looks for coming in late to the service.

Recreation—Let's face it. The body of a teenager is comprised of materials NASA engineers would kill to get their hands on. They bounce, they bend, and when the law of gravity rears its ugly head, they heal at remarkable rates. This considered, it stands to reason that teens can enjoy activities which would put an adult in traction.

What amazes me is how an otherwise healthy, active teenager doesn't have the strength necessary to walk the quarter mile to school each morning. Yet let the bell ring at three o'clock and Lazarus comes to life. That previously lethargic adolescent runs the length of the basketball court, from net to net and back again. Puzzling, that's all I can say.

Now, admittedly, this list falls far short of complete, and I won't begin to pretend that I have covered every pertinent subject. Consider it a "starter," something to get conversation moving and the creative parental juices flowing as you begin your own support group. Feel free to come up with your own discussion topics or borrow freely from those listed above.

Above all, when things get hectic, remember, you are not alone; there is sanity in numbers. We remain here to support and encourage you. We are one. We are PESTs.

My dear children,
for whom I am again in the pains of childbirth until Christ is
formed in you, how I wish I could be with you now and change
my tone, because I am perplexed about you!
Galatians 4:19–20

THIRTEEN

The Family Coach

As a tuned-in, totally aware parent of the nineties, I look for the subtle hints that indicate a crisis in our children's lives—the slight personality changes, the quiet little whispers of a problem. One evening I was evaluating the contents of the refrigerator when my son arrived home early from football practice. He slammed the front door, threw his notebook across the room, and screamed something about ignorant primates as he passed by the kitchen. Two questions sprang immediately to mind: First, how can a kid taking five subjects own only one school book? and second, is that Jello mold still any good? My wife came up with a different question.

"Is something bothering you, Dear?" she asked.

"Just wondering if that Jello mold is any good," I answered.

"I was talking to our son." She glared at me with that you're-an-insensitive-lout look that I know so well, and I took it to mean that the Jello had not yet reached its half-life.

As I continued the inventory of the refrigerator's contents, Ron made a second pass at the kitchen, coming to rest in the center of the room just as I ruled out the crisper drawer. He stood motionless, feet shoulder length apart, hands on his hips. Years of fathering skills kicked in, and I realized he wanted to talk.

"What do you know about this Jello mold?" I asked. "And why do they call it a mold, anyway? Does it have something to do with the container you make it in or do they use some sort of fungus to get it to stick together? Yeast, maybe? Yeah, I bet it's yeast." His lack of a response indicated that he knew as little about Jello as I did, and an awkward silence followed before he changed the subject (teenagers hate to admit they don't know something).

"Dad, I want you to talk to my football coach."

I was accustomed to hearing things like "You have to talk to my English teacher" or "The principal requests the honor of your presence," but some years had passed since one of my children *wanted* me to contact a school official. I probed for more information.

"Excuse me, did you say you want me to talk to your football coach?"

"Yes."

"Correct me if I'm wrong, but wouldn't that blow this whole orphan thing you've got going? I mean, it would be like admitting you have parents. No more walking ten yards in front of us at the mall, no denying that you know us. Are you ready to take that risk?"

"Dad, I'm not in the mood."

"OK, Son, I apologize. Why do you want me to talk to the coach?"

"He's not fair. He's a jerk. He hates me, and he cut me from the team!"

My heart broke for Ron; making the team meant a lot to him. I wanted to agree. I wanted to believe the coach was a jerk and just didn't like my son, but having heard these words before, I knew better. *He's not fair* pertained to most authority figures. *He's a jerk* meant my son was in disagreement with his opinion. And *He hates me . . .* well, so did the lunchroom attendant, principal, and the guy that gave him his first driving test. Ron was in need, however, and it was the latter part of his statement I chose to address.

"I'm sorry he cut you, Ron. I know how hard you tried."

"Are you going to talk to him?"

"What would you like me to say?"

"I don't believe it," he ranted. "This is just like you. You say you're there for me, but when it comes down to it, you're not."

"Son, if you really want me to talk to your coach, I will. But don't you think it would be better to talk to him yourself? Did you ask him why he cut you? Is it possible he had a reason?"

"I told you, he just doesn't like me. He said I was too small. I'm nearly six feet!"

"Ron, I'm not saying you're wrong, but think for a minute. Is it possible that height isn't what he was talking about? You tried out for linebacker, Son. How many 120-pound linebackers do you see in the NFL? Maybe you should consider playing receiver."

"I can't catch."

"How about running back?"

"Too slow."

"Quarter—"

"Can't throw," he interrupted.

"Ron, I know this might seem like a silly question, but if you know you can't run, throw, or catch, why did you try out for football?"

"I wanted a varsity letter. You got a letter for football when you were in school."

"Things were different for me, Ron, and I had a hard time too."

"Did you know your father had a nickname when he was with the team?" my wife chimed in. I had hoped she wouldn't remember. "They called him 'Slide Rule.' Tell him how you got the name, Darling."

"It was because you always got the extra few inches, wasn't it, Dad?"

"Not exactly."

"Go ahead. Tell him, Dear. Your father played special teams." Sue appeared to be enjoying herself immensely.

"Well, you see, Ron, I didn't exactly make the cut . . . not at first anyway. And then a couple of the star players started failing algebra, and the coach sort of made me a . . . special teams guy."

"What kind of a special teams guy, Dad?"

"Kind of a math tutor, I guess. My job was to make sure everyone passed their math classes. But, I got to play a little too."

"Twice, wasn't it? They were really far ahead," my wife added.

I stood there silently, mulling over my wedding vows and trying to think of something comforting to say to our son. Nothing all that comforting came to mind.

"Ron, take the evening to think about your goals," I said. "Maybe you can find another sport to letter in. For that matter, try to decide if a letter is really that important. If you still want me to talk to your coach, I will. But I don't think there's anything I can say to him that you couldn't say better."

Our son was late getting home from school the next day and upon entering the house, slammed the front door and dropped his schoolbooks in the middle of the kitchen table—

not perfect, yet a noticeable improvement from the day before.

"Mom, Dad, good news," he beamed. "I took Dad's advice and talked to the coach. He's gonna give me another shot."

"That's great, Ron!" we sang in unison.

"Linebacker?" I asked.

"No, chemistry. The quarterback is having a real tough time with the table of elements. But at least I'll get to play once in a while, and I'll get my letter—that is, if the quarterback gets his."

"That's great. I'm proud of you, Son. A real chip off the old block."

"Thanks, Dad. Well, gotta run. I need to study my chemistry."

My boy, the athlete. Makes a father proud.

Are all apostles? Are all prophets? Are all teachers?
Do all work miracles? Do all have gifts of healing?
Do all speak in tongues? Do all interpret?
But eagerly desire the greater gifts.
And now I will show you the most excellent way.

1 Corinthians 12:29–31

FOURTEEN

The Set Up

Dad, I've got a favor to ask you, and I want you to hear me out before you say no," my son said.

Instinctively, I reached into my back pocket and shoved my wallet down securely. "Sure, Ron. Go ahead."

"Remember that party some of us were planning to have over at Jeff Wheeler's in a couple of weeks? The all-nighter with a band and everything?

"No, I can't say that I do, but go on."

"Well, there seems to be a problem with the location all of a sudden, and we were wondering if we could have it here."

"What happened with the Wheeler's?" I asked as my hand reflexively released my wallet and started hunting for the house keys.

"Jeff's father said he still hasn't got the bathroom door re-hung from the last party and chances weren't too good for having another one soon—something about pigs flying and snowballs in July."

"You aren't planning a career in sales, by chance?" I asked.

"Uh-uh, why?"

"Never mind. Go on."

"There would be just a few of us, and you and Mom wouldn't have to do a thing. We'd take care of getting the house ready and cleaning up afterwards. No sweat."

"Is that it?" I asked.

"Pretty much," he said. "There's just one other small thing. I'd like you and Mom to be somewhere else."

I was caught slightly off-guard by the last request and decided to seek clarification. "Somewhere else?"

He nodded.

"Are you referring to somewhere else as in another room of the house, or somewhere else as in Kansas?"

"Don't take it personally, Dad," he said. "I just know how much you and Mom like to spend time alone, and I thought this would be a perfect time to go on a cruise or something. That way we wouldn't bother you."

A better man would have been grateful, having raised such a selfless child, but alas, I am not a better man. "So you're doing this for us?"

"No, not completely. But we might as well make the best of the situation, right?"

There was a long pause before I spoke. I wanted to choose my words carefully, so as to not offend. "Is my scar showing?" I asked.

"What scar, Dad?"

"From the lobotomy," I answered. "You are obviously under the impression that someone has hacked out a sizable portion of my brain."

"I just thought you were receding."

"I am not receding," I said, suddenly feeling defensive, "and I think you're missing the point. Do you really think we're going to leave the house unsupervised while several hundred teenagers run amuck?"

"There won't be several hundred, Dad. Maybe twenty at most—and their dates."

"And whoever else finds out about it," I said.

"We'll keep it quiet, Dad. I promise."

"Ron, forty teenagers couldn't keep the Manhattan Project a secret. Do you mean to tell me that you don't expect any uninvited guests?"

"I'll handle it, Dad."

"I'm sorry, Ron, but your mother and I have worked hard to put together this home, and I don't feel comfortable leaving it unsupervised under those conditions."

"So you don't trust me, is that it?"

"Of course I trust you," I explained. "It's not a matter of trusting you, but how can you expect to control the actions of that many people? I'm sorry, but I'm not comfortable with this."

"Grandma let you and Uncle Jimmy have parties all the time, and the police had to come and break those up."

"Where did you hear that?" I asked, painfully remembering the details.

"Grandma told me about it. She said she even had to drain the swimming pool because one of your friends dumped a gallon of hair dye in it."

"What is this, some sort of 'rite of passage' thing?" I asked. "Because I supposedly—and I stress supposedly—trashed my parents' home, I'm obligated to allow you the same opportunity?"

"You always say I should be responsible, but you don't want to give me a chance to prove that I am."

"Listen," I tried to reason, "maybe we can reach a compromise. How about inviting a few less teenagers and a couple more adults—I have two in mind. And maybe you could drop the band. If you're willing to start small, I'll work with you. Don't try to re-create Woodstock at your first party."

"Woodstock?"

"It was a big party; it's not important."

"How many can I invite?" he asked, showing an unusual willingness to barter.

"Ten sounds good," I said, "total."

"How about twenty, Dad, and you and Mom stay at the neighbors?"

"Twenty, and Mom and I will lock ourselves in the bedroom. And you agree to have your friends out by midnight."

"What if you and Mom go over to the neighbors and just stop by once in a while to check things out?"

"I'll think about it," I answered. "You do understand, however, that this agreement is not binding until further management approval is received?"

"You mean Mom, right?"

"I mean Mom, right."

For a brief moment I felt good, as if we had actually come to an agreement that all parties could live with. But as is often the case with teenagers, the other shoe was about to drop.

"Grandma, the envelope please," my son yelled, a smile from ear to ear.

His grandmother walked into the room with a sealed envelope, the word *Dad* on the front. I opened it cautiously, knowing by their faces that it could only be bad news. Written across the single page inside were the words: *twenty guests, limited supervision.*

"I think I've been had," I said, beginning to detect a conspiracy in my home. "How did you know I'd agree to this?"

Still sporting the ear-to-ear grin, Ron answered, "Grandma told me I should always ask big and leave plenty of room to bargain."

"Your grandmother should have been a teamster," I said, wondering how Jimmy Hoffa might have handled the competition. "Why is it," I asked, turning to my mother, "that I didn't turn out smarter than my parents or my children? It strikes me as a little unfair."

"Well, you know how it is," she answered. "Some things skip a generation."

The father of a righteous man has great joy;
he who has a wise son delights in him.
May your father and mother be glad;
may she who gave you birth rejoice!

Proverbs 23:24–25

FIFTEEN

Me Doth Protest Too Much, She Thinks

Several months ago, Sue and I, along with several couples we may never see again, suffered through an evening out at the California Shakespeare festival. For the record, neither I, nor a single one of my male counterparts went willingly. Arguing on biblical grounds that nothing good can come from a group of men wearing tights, we attempted to boycott the evening altogether. Since our wives had conveniently purchased non-refundable tickets, as well as the team of wild horses necessary to drag us along, we consented after some heated debate to make the best of it.

If you happen to be one of those nine or ten people who find Shakespeare riveting, you have my condolences. As for me, nothing less than declaring the site ground zero for a post-SALT nuclear test could have saved the evening. While dividing my time between naps and rubbing the sore spot where Sue kept elbowing me, I managed to find a few moments to read the literature they handed out before some fiend set about bolting the doors and trapping us inside the theater.

I'm going out on a limb here and assuming that every couple received the information pack, and we were not singled out for our choice of attire (blue jeans and T-shirts — our tuxedos were in the shop). Some thoughtful soul, in a useless, though gallant, attempt to rescue a portion of our evening, took the time to outline each scene, act by act, character by character, and summarize the entire play in writing. This equipped even the most culturally impaired among us to stand around with the cappuccino and latte crowd during intermission and participate in deep, meaningful conversations about such things as symbolism and the author's intended meaning.

"I believe 'The Bard' meant Hamlet to represent the inner struggle man faces between paternal loyalties and the identity of self in a world completely devoid of passion and truth," spouted one decaf-swilling patron. "What are your thoughts, gentlemen?"

"Cool sword," my friend Jerry answered, "really cool. After all these years, you think they could have finished translating the dialogue into English, though." Our caffeine-conscious friend found Jerry's poignant observations so captivating that he left us to share the comments with a few others. Obviously intimidated by our capacity for Shakespeare, nobody approached us for the remainder of the evening, and we were left to share our insights amongst ourselves.

I found it incredibly easy to block the majority of the play completely from my mind by the time we reached the parking lot, but one item stuck in my head. The cheat-sheet they provided came in handy, and had I possessed any inclination to pay attention to what transpired on stage, it would have proved downright beneficial. That got me to thinking, which I do on occasion, how helpful a list like that might be for the local church. Seekers and new Christians would be given a program explaining the roles of their congregation's major players and some definitions of commonly used terms and phrases. No more would a young Christian feel intimidated and afraid to speak; the barrier of jargon would be overcome. People would feel more at home.

Always ready to further the cause of Christ through the written word, I have accepted the awesome responsibility of providing a first draft—a dictionary of sorts—aimed at defining those terms and positions common to Christian churches in general. I offer this lexicon here first for your inspection. Every attempt has been made to avoid denominational bias, doctrinal prejudice, and, in most cases, theological relevance. Feel free to forward any additions directly to my attention for consideration in the final release.

The Cast of Characters:

Pastor A minister charged with ensuring the spiritual growth of a congregation or worship group. Often confused for a "Sundays Only" employee, the pastor reaps such benefits as an eighty-hour work week, meager financial remuneration, and the opportunity to listen attentively to various complaints. Many pastors enjoy additional job responsibilities as janitor, maintenance man, and landscape architect for their given congregation.

Youth Pastor Responsibilities similar to those of pastor but focused on the student population. Youth pastors are frequently young, healthy men of God, capable of withstanding extreme physical punishment in their attempts to keep up with their charges. Look for a man with glazed eyes, a nervous twitch, and thirty teenagers in tow.

Business Manager Accountant or administrative staff member sometimes hired by larger congregations to free the pastor from fits of depression caused by attempting to pay salaries and purchase luxuries for the church like Bibles, heating oil, and electricity. Good business managers possess the gift of miracles, sometimes manifested in the form of paying for Bibles, heating oil, and electricity with seemingly insufficient resources.

Deacon One of a group of members chosen for their proven character and inability to run quickly enough when asked to serve. Tasked by biblical ordinance to aid and assist the pastoral staff, deacons help with various business and spiritual matters like intercepting letters addressed "Dear Heretic" and resolving serious congregational disputes ("I've sat right in that same spot for thirty years and now she comes along and thinks she can park herself anywhere she pleases!").

Layperson Not to be confused with the person asleep in the pew next to you, laymen (or laywomen, laypeople?) are those members and attendees not a part of the organized clergy.

Volunteer Any layperson who willingly gives of his or her time in service to God and His people. Pastors' wives rank among the most consistent and sometimes unwitting volunteers ("As I'm sure the pastor's wife would love to lead the clothing drive, I've taken the liberty of putting her phone number on the flyers").

Definition of Terms:

Tithe   Archaic term once used to denote a tenth of one's income, especially in reference to charitable contributions or money given as an offering to God. In recent years, common usage and incredibly poor math skills on the part of some parishioners have served to broaden the meaning to encompass amounts ranging from the original 10 percent to whatever happens to be left over at the end of a given pay period. Example: "Hey, Martha, have you paid the cable bill yet, and do you think we'll have enough left over for a tithe?"

Gossip   A detestable habit of spreading rumors, partial truths, or sensational talk of a personal or confidential nature. Often preceded by statements such as: "You know I'm not one to gossip, but . . . ," "Now I really shouldn't be telling you this . . . ," and "I'm only mentioning this so that you can pray for him."

Sometimes known as "Praise Gossip," a particularly reprehensible form may be overheard during group prayer sessions. Example: ". . . and thank you, Lord, that Martha's no-good, cheating husband Earl isn't stepping out with that blonde tramp down at the Quick-Mart anymore."

Dance   Denounced by some denominations as an evil and sinful practice, leading to lust and other sins of the flesh, dance is defined as moving rhythmically—usually in time to accompanying music. Note: not to be confused with "Expressive Motion" or "Worship Movements," also moving rhythmically and in time to accompanying music, but in a sanctuary or worship setting.

Sermon A thirty to forty-five minute discourse in which a pastor attempts to overcome a variety of distractions (babies crying, latecomers finding seats, etc.) while transferring God's message to his flock. Contrary to popular belief, good sermons don't necessarily go hand-in-hand with good congregational response, many preferring an uplifting pep talk to a convicting exhortation. Among those statements rarely heard by pastors: "Great sermon, Pastor. You should speak on stewardship every Sunday!"

Retreat A weekend or occasionally week-long trip away from the rigors of daily life for the purpose of spiritual rest or enrichment. Also what the pastor does following the closing remarks of his annual stewardship sermon.

Church Bus Mythical form of transportation occasionally rumored to be in full working order. Church buses, unlike other forms of mass transportation, are not intended so much for moving people as for building faith in the faint of heart. ("Do you trust Jesus, Harold?" "Yes, Pastor. I do." "Good, Harold, then get on the church bus.")

Challenge Synonymous with "difficult," challenge is used to soften the blow when an impending task appears particularly burdensome. As in: "This could be a real challenge for you."

Great Commission   Not the money some unscrupulous televangelists take home each week, the Great Commission, outlined in Matthew 28:19, instructs us to "go out and make disciples"—sometimes misinterpreted as the Great Suggestion.

While this work, admittedly, serves to define only a minor sampling of Christian offices and jargon, the author hopes it will prove useful. Suggested additions and positive comments regarding the preceding content may be forwarded in care of the author to the publisher's address. Criticism and complaints of various nature should be forwarded directly to the California Shakespeare society.

As the rain and the snow come down from heaven,
and do not return to it without watering the earth and making
it bud and flourish, so that it yields seed for the sower and bread
for the eater, so is my word that goes out from my mouth: It will
not return to me empty, but will accomplish what I desire and
achieve the purpose for which I sent it.

Isaiah 55:10–11

SIXTEEN

Ode to Beatrice Pennybaker

Common belief among the majority of elementary-age children holds that some teachers (an archaic word since replaced by "educators") actually enter the profession for no better reason than to enjoy a free rein in inflicting various forms of mental torture on the defenseless and burgeoning minds of our nation's youth. This theory quickly falls apart when students enter high school and realize that it is they who enjoy a free rein, and the inflicting of mental torture takes a serious turn for the worse, now aimed at the defenseless and already bludgeoned minds of our nation's educators. Teaching can be a difficult and trying profession.

Now separated from my years as a student by the ever-increasing buffer of time, I realize that most teachers are no different than you or I. They are simply average citizens trying to make a decent living who managed to wrangle a job that includes roughly three months of vacation time each year. While this, in itself, is reason enough to hold the entire teaching profession in disdain, it doesn't begin to explain anomalies like Mrs. Pennybaker, my sixth-grade teacher and possibly the meanest woman I ever met.

Being sentenced to Mrs. Pennybaker's classroom for a term of nine months was generally viewed with the same enthusiasm as being drafted in the armed forces—without the benefit of a neat-looking uniform. Unlike today's educators, she wasn't burdened with any philosophical frills aimed at making the learning experience a sharing process. Learning was not so much a process as a drill to be repeated, and Mrs. P. repeated these drills with all the zeal and enthusiasm of the best forced-labor camp commandant.

On the first day of school, I made a solemn promise to draw as little attention to myself as humanly possible. I'd go to school, complete my assignments, and hope for an early parole, or at the very worst, release following time served. Under no circumstances would I draw unnecessary attention and risk extending my sentence. Quiet and unassuming became my new middle names.

Whether or not Mrs. Pennybaker ever got around to learning my middle names, I'll never know. She did, however, pick up on my first and last names right away—a point that probably should have flattered me, but rather served to scare me half to death. Within the first ten minutes of her class— and through no fault of my own, I might add—I found myself seated between two primary combatants in the opening day spitball war to end all spitball wars.

Remembering my pledge to remain quiet and unassuming, I refrained from joining in the festivities for a record-breaking three minutes, at which point a stray round from the belligerent on my left entered my ear and traveled a considerable distance toward my brain. Temporarily lapsing into a state of semiconsciousness known as stupidity, I grabbed my straw and laid down a barrage of purely defensive fire in two directions. Not that I wanted to engage in such tomfoolery, you understand; I did it solely for the preservation of honor. That I happened to be in the possession of a straw at that unusual hour of the day was strictly coincidental, and goes to show you how bad things sometimes happen to good people. As fate had it, Mrs. Pennybaker chose that particular moment to turn her head in my direction and proceed with the furthering of our acquaintance.

"Achtung!" she yelled from her station at the front of the room. "So, we have a little troublemaker, do we? Good, good! It's nice to have examples for our first day." She marched toward me in modified goosestep, pausing for effect just inches in front of my desk. "Give me your hand, Mr. Spit-wad. We have something for little troublemakers."

A voice inside of me was yelling "run! run!" or possibly it was the whispered voices next to me; it's all a blur. I stuck out my left hand (non-pitching, of course) and wondered for a brief moment what she had in mind. Not one to leave flies tied up in her web for all that long, Mrs. Pennybaker dazzled the class with her display of speed and agility.

Seemingly out of nowhere, she produced a ruler of immense proportion, the likes of which have since been outlawed by the Department of Weights and Measures. With quick, successive flicks of the wrist, she brought the mighty beam down on my knuckles three or four times and holstered the deadly weapon before I or anyone else saw where it went or, for that matter, from whence it came. My vision may have been impaired slightly from the presence of moisture in my eyes. The other students were too busy laughing to provide solid clues.

I know you must be shocked that such a blatant display of violence could take place in our nation's classrooms. Believe me, so was I. But you must remember that this incident occurred during the dark ages of public education, back when corporal punishment was the norm and teachers were supposed to be better armed than the students. Rest assured, corporal punishment is a thing of the past, as is the associated response: every student's complete and undivided attention.

The ruler episode turned out to be one of the nicest moments Mrs. Pennybaker and I would share. Had we found some common ground early on, things might have worked out better. But as it turned out, Mrs. P. had some rather unreasonable expectations where my education was concerned, namely, she intended for me to obtain one, and this was contrary to some of my deepest, most heartfelt beliefs.

I had no problem with learning as a general concept, just so long as the subject promised to provide me with a skill or knowledge I felt might come in handy some day. If Mrs. Pennybaker taught physical education, she would have found me more attentive. But Beatrice Pennybaker loved literature, and of all the genres available to choose from, poetry found its place in her heart. I, along with the majority of my classmates, thought her heart a fitting place for poetry and wished she would have kept it there for the remainder of her days—if not, at the very least, for the remainder of our days together.

Each morning, class began with a mandatory reading from the collected works of a variety of poets—all with some local connection. Her favorite was Walt Whitman, a man born in Huntington, Long Island, who later moved to Brooklyn. As best I could tell from reading his poetry, Walt was a confused, delusional man, and a mighty poor communicator as well. With his poem "When Lilacs Last in the Dooryard Bloom'd" he took an entire eight pages to express sorrow over the death of President Lincoln, and we only figured that out when Mrs. P. broke down and gave us the answer. Never once did the guy mention Lincoln by name, which would have saved us all considerable aggravation and a good deal of time.

Had Mrs. Pennybaker been satisfied with reading the poetry to us and leaving well enough alone, things might have gone OK. Not one to stifle the spirit of class participation, however, Mrs. P. developed the habit of asking for volunteers each morning to read the day's selection. All of the feminine names on her roster were exhausted during the first ten days. Day eleven held little promise for finding a willing volunteer.

"Who would like to read today's poem?" Mrs. Pennybaker asked. She qualified her statement with the dreaded, though inevitable phrase, "Someone who hasn't read yet." Every boy in the class immediately launched into his own diversion technique, designed to make himself appear an undesirable prospect for the assignment at hand. Avoiding eye contact was the first rule, another common practice involved brushing papers or pencils to the floor and collecting them in a slow, methodical manner. Raised by parents who emphasized politeness, I tried the direct approach.

"No thank you, Ma'am," I said, with all the politeness I could muster. "Maybe some other time."

"No thank you?" Mrs. Pennybaker questioned. "No thank you? And why not, may I ask?" Invoking an age-old motivational tool known as intimidation, Mrs. P. followed up with another question. "You can read, can't you?"

"Sure I can read," I answered.

"Then why don't you care to read from Walt Whitman?" she asked. "Don't you like poetry?"

At this point I began to wonder about Mrs. Pennybaker's credentials and what, if anything, qualified her to teach. She asked a lot of questions for someone with a college education, the answers to which appeared fairly obvious to me. Switching tacks from politeness to honesty, I offered my response. "No, Ma'am. I don't like it one bit."

This apparently wasn't the answer she was looking for, I determined, in part by the look of disgust which enveloped her and later by the punishment she handed out.

"One should never determine that one doesn't like something, young man," Mrs. Pennybaker lectured, "until one has studied the subject long enough to comprehend its entire meaning. Do you understand what I'm telling you?"

"No, Ma'am," I answered.

"What I'm trying to say, Mr. Darbee, is that you don't enjoy poetry because you fail to understand its hidden meanings. Now do you follow me?"

"I'm sorry, Ma'am," I said, "but I don't like broccoli either, and I figure I understand it just as well as the next guy."

Had I known Mrs. Pennybaker held broccoli in such high regard, I would have said cauliflower, but it was too late. Mrs. P. turned beet red—another vegetable I could have chosen—and goose-stepped to the edge of my desk.

"Maybe I can help you to develop a better understanding, Mr. Darbee," she threatened. Instinctively, both of my hands found their way deep into my pockets as I prepared myself for the emergence of the ruler. "I believe I have the perfect assignment for you."

Hoping to expand my mind, Mrs. Pennybaker ordered me to write my own metrical composition of at least eight lines detailing my thoughts and feelings regarding poetry. I almost didn't believe a woman could be so cruel, but rather than argue over the assignment and risk another engagement with the ruler, I accepted my fate with great resignation.

That evening, I sat at the kitchen table and attempted to craft a poem that suitably described my thoughts and feelings. I briefly contemplated writing a scathing piece attacking Mrs. Pennybaker's character and overall sense of compassion but wisely refrained. Instead, I found what I believed to be inarguable justification for my opinions in the opening lines of Genesis. Moments later, I completed my assignment and packed it away in my school bag.

The next morning, Mrs. Pennybaker opened the class with the pledge of allegiance and turned toward me, ruler in hand. "Have we completed our assignment, Mr. Troublemaker?" she asked.

"Yes, Ma'am," I answered.

"Then would you like to stand up and read it to the class?"

Remembering from my previous experience that Mrs. P. held certain preconceived notions as to what I should and shouldn't like to do, I answered affirmatively.

Standing at my place in the back row, I opened my notebook and extracted the results of my efforts. With a nervous look to my surrounding peers, I cleared my throat and began to read:

> God created the heavens and all of the earth
> Spoke it into existence, gave creation its birth.
> From the biblical records I'm able to find
> He didn't use meter, lyric, or rhyme.
> So while I am sure that your motives are good
> I see no valid reason this poetry should
> cause as much aggravation as is already done.
> Let us move on to something a little more fun.

Whether she was impressed by my grasp of theology or simply amazed I had completed the assignment, Mrs. P. accepted my work and allowed me to take my seat. She was quiet for some time and instructed us to behave likewise and read silently at our desks.

That turned out to be the last poem I read in my year of sixth grade, and Mrs. Pennybaker stopped reading them to us. I guess she figured that if God chose clear and direct communication for something as important as creation, she probably wasn't in a position to argue.

Occasionally, I wonder what became of Mrs. Pennybaker. She retired after that year, and we never heard from her again. It's funny how the most unlikely people can impact your life. I think about her often when I stumble across a particularly bad greeting card or pick up a ruler. I wonder if she still thinks about me.

In the beginning God created the heavens and the earth.
Now the earth was formless and empty,
darkness was over the surface of the deep,
and the Spirit of God was hovering over the waters.
And God said, "Let there be light," and there was light.

Genesis 1:1–3

SEVENTEEN

When Your Prayer Life Is Heading Downhill

The mother of my boyhood friend and companion, Anthony Gianelli, was one of the most prayerful women I ever met. Never farther than a dash and a grab away from the nearest rosary, Mrs. Gianelli was to practicing Catholics what Dr. Pasteur was to practicing physicians. Not having the benefit of a Catholic upbringing, as Mrs. Gianelli put it, I found myself a little confused by the rosary and the significance it held for her. One afternoon, as Tony and I scoured the streets for new additions to our bottlecap collection, I probed the subject with a few carefully calculated questions.

"Hey, Tony," I said, mustering my courage. "I gotta ask you something, and you gotta promise not to repeat it, OK?"

"That depends. What's it worth to ya?"

"Cut it out. I'm serious. You can't say anything to anybody."

"OK, shoot."

"Do I look like a girl to you?" I asked. "I mean if you didn't know me and you walked into me at school, would you think I was a girl?"

Tony stopped short and looked up from his scouring position. "What color dress would you be wearin', if I bumped into you at school, I mean?"

"Quit it. I'm not kiddin' around. Just answer the question."

"No, you don't look like a girl. What's the matter with you, anyway? Even if you wore a dress to school and let your hair grow real long, you're too ugly to be a girl."

"Thanks, Tony," I said. He was a fountain of affirmation. "But if I don't look like a girl, then why's your mom always calling me Mary Fullagrace?"

"What are you talking about?"

"Your mom. Every time I come over she says 'Hail, Mary Fullagrace' like some Roman centurion and grabs for one of those beaded necklaces she's got stashed around the house. Kinda makes a guy feel strange, always being mistaken for a girl and all."

"That's 'Hail, Mary, full of grace' you idgit. Ain't you never seen nobody pray the rosary before?"

Pausing briefly to straighten out the negatives in Tony's statement, I answered, "I don't know. Yeah, sure. I guess so. So why does she pray when I come to the door?"

"Don't worry about it. It's not you. She gets worried anytime I'm hangin' around with somebody. She's afraid I'm gonna get hurt or do somethin' stupid."

This was understandable, seeing as how I harbored the same fears whenever we were together, with possibly a tad of that selfish self-preservation instinct mixed in for good measure. Tony's mind was completely devoid of anything resembling common sense when it came to trying something new or dangerous. He never backed away from a dare and usually went a little farther than required, just for effect. In fact, most kids had stopped daring him to do anything out of fear they would sustain injury in the process or, at the least, face charges for his wrongful death.

Feeling more secure in my masculinity, thanks to Tony's explanation, we went home to empty our pockets. Mr. Gianelli called out his customary greeting as we entered the front door. "Hey, Angela! Guess who's home? Told ya he ain't dead."

Mrs. Gianelli came in through the kitchen, rosary in one hand, first-aid kit in the other. Following a quick spot check, which included a summary counting of fingers and toes, Tony's mom put away the medical supplies and we headed for his room, the clicking of rosary beads fading into the distance.

"This is your lucky day," Tony said as we deposited our bottlecaps in the empty coffee can that housed our collection. "I'm about to let you in on the ground floor of my newest project."

A cold chill ran up my spine and apparently froze my brain, because I failed to bolt from the room screaming in the manner I promised myself I would after experiencing the last ground-floor opportunity. As I mentioned earlier, Tony had a flair for the dangerous. This flair sometimes manifested itself in unexpected ways, wherein Tony turned common household products into class-1 pyrotechnics and children's toys into weapons of mass destruction.

Regaining my composure, if not my senses, I folded my arms and planted my feet at shoulder-width, determined to make a stand. "Sounds great!" I said. "Let's see it." (I was not a terribly strong-willed child.)

Opening the closet door, Tony retrieved a long cardboard tube, such as one would expect to contain blueprints or engineering drawings. "I got the plans right here," he said, holding the cylinder proudly, like the anchor man in a relay race displaying the baton. The professional packaging lost a degree of its effect, however, when Tony uncapped the tube and poured out his plans, a handful of baseball card wrappers marked with sketches of a mechanical nature.

"Neat!" I said, which is what every kid my age said when at a loss for a more descriptive term. "Sort of looks like a cage with wheels. What's it do?"

"It flies," Tony answered. Briefly overtaken by another cold chill, I waited for further explanation. "This here's the fastest shopping cart racer this side of the Hudson," he explained. "We're gonna have ourselves a Shopping Cart Derby, and everybody'll come from all over to watch us race down *The Hill.*"

The Hill! Legend had it some deranged city planner ordered the highway department to take a left when they should have been heading right and a six-story brownstone had been covered with asphalt in the process, thus *The Hill.* The series of cold chills that followed prompted me to swear off popsicles for weeks to come.

"Maybe *The Hill* is a little steep for our first race," I said, trying not to sound terrified. "You think maybe we should start off on something flat first?"

"No way. That's the beauty of it," he said. "The cage will protect you if you run into any cars or anything."

"You mean if *you* run into any cars or anything," I said.

"No, I mean you. I'm kinda what you'd call the behind-the-scenes inventor type. By gettin' in on the ground floor, you get to take the maiden voyage. You know I'd really like to be in there with you, but I gotta stay behind in case of any mechanical problems. You're not scared of a little shopping cart, are you? You ain't gonna chicken out?"

Assuring Tony that I certainly wasn't afraid of any old shopping cart, we headed for the market to pick out a quality cruiser. Looking for any opportunity to call this adventure off, short of admitting cowardice, I questioned Tony on the ethics of acquiring a shopping cart. "Won't this be like stealing?" I asked as we searched for a cart with four good wheels.

"What's it say right here on the handle?" Tony asked.

"For your convenience," I read.

"That means we can do what we want with it. They put these here for our convenience. It's the same as one of them 'Take one' signs they got with the handouts by the register."

The question of ethics now behind us, we spent the next thirty minutes trying to find a cart capable of sustaining forward motion without jerking to one side or the other. As those familiar with shopping can testify, they are a rare commodity. Eventually, we settled on a fine metal chariot and pushed it to the alley behind Tony's house to begin the transformation.

Following his plan to the letter, we used a hacksaw to remove the metal supports suspending the cart above the wheels. Some thick baling wire, originally used to bundle newspapers, served to reconnect the cage to the bottom frame and wheels. (The low center of gravity we achieved would provide an added edge in speed, Tony lectured.) To cut our wind resistance, we attached plywood to the sides and a rear spoiler. The cart appeared ready to race, but looked too much like a rolling coffin for my liking.

"What do ya think?" Tony asked, staring proudly at our creation. "Ready to climb aboard?"

"I don't know, Tony. Looks a little flimsy down by the wheels. Maybe we should use something stronger than wire."

"Don't go gettin' crazy on me," Tony said. "You want a little play in the wheels; it's called suspension. Gives you a smoother ride."

"You know, I've been thinking," I said, "maybe we should test drive this thing together, unless you're afraid or somethin'."

"I told you, I gotta stay behind in case of any mechanical problems."

"That's my point," I argued. "Wouldn't it be better if you were in the cart to take care of the problems—of course, nobody would blame you for bein' scared."

"I ain't afraid of nothin'. You just scoot down in back, cause I'm riding with you."

My memory gets a little fuzzy at this point, possibly resulting from a protection mechanism God put into our brains or the concussion I suffered—either way I'll try to outline the events as best I can recall.

We climbed into the cart from above, Tony claiming the dominant position in the front. Almost instantly, the law of gravity reared its ugly head, and the metal racer began its ill-fated descent. Picking up momentum at what I later estimated to be a new land-speed record, a crucial flaw in Tony's engineering strategy became apparent.

"We're going too fast!" I yelled. "Put on the brakes!"

"We don't have any brakes!" Tony yelled back.

What we also didn't have was steering, outside of our ability to shift weight and influence the general bearing of the cart. Screaming for all we were worth, we continued our rapid descent toward the bottom of the hill, leaning left and right as the need arose to keep us in the street.

"AAAaaaahhhhhhhh!" I screamed, as we zipped past the kosher deli.

"AAAaaaahhhhhhhh!" Tony responded, as we raced by his mother, shopping at the local fruit stand. Mrs. Gianelli shouted something in return, and even with a limited grasp of the Italian language, I was able to catch the gist of her message by the sign of the cross she gestured and the blur of rosary beads.

Yet another engineering flaw became evident at this moment, as we hit a manhole cover and momentarily achieved flight. Flight was not our primary worry, though certain aspects of landing posed a direct concern. As the cart entered its upward trajectory, the wheels continued to go forward, blowing huge holes in Tony's baling wire theory.

"AAAaaaahhhhhhhh!" I screamed, just in case Tony missed it the first time.

"AAAaaaahhhhhhhh!" he returned.

Hitting the pavement with only the upper portion of our vehicle intact, we skidded the better part of thirty feet before coming to a quiet and restful stop courtesy of a parked Plymouth sedan. The fender broke our fall rather nicely, tearing away Tony's final engineering myth regarding the protection afforded by our craft's cage.

Drifting pleasantly in and out of consciousness, I found comfort in the sight of Tony's parents hovering over us. The last thing I heard before blacking out was the comforting words of Mr. Gianelli: "See, Angela! It's OK. They're not dead!"

Following an overnight stay for observation, Tony and I won our release from the hospital and returned to our respective homes. We were graciously awarded another day of bed rest before our parents farmed us out to reimburse the grocery store for the loss of one shopping cart.

En route to my new job as assistant floor sweeper and bag boy, I stopped by the Gianelli home to meet Tony. Knocking on the front door, I heard a shuffling noise and a familiar voice rang out, "Who's there?"

"It's me, Mrs. Gianelli," I said.

"Who's me?"

"Me, Mrs. Gianelli—Tony's friend. You know . . . Mary Fullagrace?"

A minute or so passed, and when the door opened, Tony's father filled the opening.

"He'll be right out," Mr. Gianelli said. "You want to come in or wait here?"

"I'll wait here, thank you," I answered.

"Probably a good idea," Mr. Gianelli said. "So what do they got you boys doing to work off the money?"

"I'm gonna sweep floors and bag groceries," I answered. "Tony's gonna work in the back with the butcher." A loud wailing sound emanated from the living room following my comment, along with the now familiar clicking of beads.

"Hail, Mary, full of grace!" Mrs. Gianelli shouted.

"Excuse me, kid," Mr. Gianelli said. "I gotta go take care of Anthony's mom. She's a little excitable. He'll be out in a minute."

As we walked down the steps, Mr. Gianelli's voice drifted through the open window. "For crying out loud, Angela, he ain't gonna die!"

I only wished I could share his optimism.

He who brings trouble on his family will inherit only wind, and the fool will be servant to the wise.

Proverbs 11:29

EIGHTEEN

It's All Just Shades of Gray

We all know that if we stick around long enough, we will get older. Yet for some reason, when it finally happens, it catches us by surprise. Like Chicago Cubs fans waiting to win a World Series, we won't be ready for it, and at best we can hope for a minimum of pain and self-induced embarrassment.

My wife, Susan, and I made a pact a number of years ago to grow old gracefully, and if at all possible, on roughly the same schedule. We're fairly safe on the graceful part since it's open to an awful lot of interpretation, and we tend to lean toward the fair-minded when making judgments that might later be turned against us. It's the schedule thing that sort of threw us for a loop around here.

Sue, possibly due to her full-time job as a mother, developed a few streaks of gray in the hair department shortly after she turned thirty-something (actual age omitted to preserve the serenity of the author's home life). She seemed to take it quite well in the beginning, all things considered, with only the minimum weeping and gnashing of teeth. Sensitive, caring guy that I am, I stepped up to the plate and tried my best to console her.

"I think it makes you look more mature," I told her in my most sensitive, caring guy voice. The glare she shot in my direction indicated that maturity was not the look she was going for. *Strike one.* I knocked the dust off the plate and leaned in for a second try.

"OK, maybe mature isn't the right word," I said. "That's not what I meant at all. Elegant! That's the word. Those little streaks of gray make you look elegant."

"Streaks!" she shot back. "So they're streaks now?" She ran to the mirror to reexamine the supposed damage. "Those are not streaks! Do you hear me?" her voice laced with tears as she shouted from the bathroom. "Just a slight dusting, nothing more." *Strike two.*

Every guy knows that when the count is 0 and 2, no choice remains but to crowd the plate and take a swing at the third pitch. Better to go down swinging for the fences than to get caught looking. "You know what, honey? I think we're letting this whole thing get a bit out of hand," I reasoned. *The pitcher winds up . . .* "Let's take a couple of deep breaths and calm down for a minute. No sense making such a fuss over something so trivial." *He releases the ball . . .* "Your mom's got all sorts of gray in her hair, and she still looks great."

Swingggg and a miss! Strike three. You're outta there! Mom comparisons are always a poor choice, but when you're behind in the count, you've got to go for broke. Side retired, I headed for the sanctuary of the study, knowing that in time, this too would pass.

It's funny how communication between a husband and wife, even when you're nearing two decades of marital bliss, can prove so difficult. When Sue and I agreed to grow old on roughly the same schedule, I took it to mean at approximately the same time, like within the same year or two. Later conversations indicated I had my signals somewhat crossed. To the best of Sue's understanding "roughly the same schedule" meant simply that as the husband, I was to age first, thus paving the way and making it easier for my lovely wife to remain graceful.

Really, though, with the exception of the initial shock, she has handled the aging process with dignity. Better than I have, if we're going to be honest about it. No doubt safer, to be sure.

Rather than face the realities of getting older head-on, as it were, I chose a more common path—denial. Professional athletes have embraced this particular tactic for years, going on to play several seasons beyond their prime. It stood to reason that if denial worked for million-dollar-a-year ballplayers, a middle-income guy like me should be able to milk it for decades. The fans certainly wouldn't notice. So, in truly adult fashion, I figured there was no reason whatsoever to accept the inevitable, just so long as I could go on ignoring it altogether.

Now, if you happen to be entertaining the idea of trying this denial thing for yourself, allow me to offer some advice. There exists a direct correlation between a person's success with denial and his or her ability to tolerate pain. This is not a venture for the fainthearted. It takes real discipline to keep your eyes from welling up with tears when your reflexes have slowed considerably and you take a sharply hit line drive in the shin.

Also, it is imperative to keep in mind that you are getting older, and continuing to treat your body as if it belonged to an eighteen-year-old triathlete may result in various parts falling off or becoming otherwise impaired. As you are likely to find those parts useful in the future, excellent medical coverage is a must for the true denial expert. A relative in the insurance business also comes in handy.

To date, I consider myself fortunate in that all my limbs remain intact and, thanks to the wonders of modern surgery, in relatively good working order. With the exception of some hair that mysteriously appears on the floor of my shower, nothing has fallen out that could not quickly be replaced. I'm also thankful for my mother's job with a medical group that doesn't mind treating me on occasion for the sheer entertainment value my injuries present.

The inevitable starts to get pretty difficult to ignore after a person's third or fourth major injury. My most recent, and I'd like to think my last, occurred when I ventured down to the church to move an organ. Actually, I went to move a piano and just happened to move an organ (internally) in the process. The resulting conversation with my doctor and the surgery that followed convinced me to face the fact I'm not a teenager any more.

"You're not a teenager any more," he said. "You'll need surgery." Subtle guy, great sense of humor—that combined with the intense pain is what keeps me coming back.

"Mind if I get a second opinion?"

"Check your birth certificate. The math is easy," he responded.

"I meant the surgery, wise guy." OK, mediocre sense of humor.

"Look," he said, poking me at the waist. "Do you see this bulge here?"

"Come on now, Doc! I wouldn't call it a bulge. A tiny spare tire, love handles maybe."

"Not that bulge, this one." He pointed to a small protrusion in my lower abdomen. "It wasn't there yesterday, and you'll be much happier if it's not there a week from now. It's a hernia. Not that unusual in a guy your age."

"If you want a second opinion," he continued, "you can schedule it right after you talk to the surgeon. By the way, he's been asking about you. What's it been, a year now?"

"You know, I could find a doctor with a real bedside manner," I reminded him.

"You could, but you'd have to start from scratch and work your way back up to the frequent-patient discount. All kidding aside, following surgery, you should start a regular program of exercise, and try to tone it down a little. Guys our age need some conditioning if we're going to try to keep up with the young ones. Think about it."

I did think about it. With four weeks convalescent leave following the surgery, I had little else to do besides think about it. Sue thought about it too. Something about me lying on the couch for weeks on end, moaning and calling her to fulfill my every need seemed to motivate her. She picked up brochures from every health club in a thirty-mile radius and sent away for information on all the latest gizmos.

We thought about something else, too.

With Sue firmly over the initial shock of her few gray hairs and me prepared to exit denial, we moved as a married couple should—hand-in-hand into the next stage of the aging process: acceptance. We're getting older, and there is absolutely nothing we can do to change that fact. Of course we can hide it and slow down the effects a bit. Sue has found a new friend in Lady Clairol, and we both started a routine of very low-impact aerobics. We may not be getting any younger, but when you consider the alternative, it's not that bad a deal.

Even when I am old and gray, do not forsake me, O God,
till I declare your power to the next generation,
your might to all who are to come.

Psalm 71:18

NINETEEN

From the Halls of Montezuma to the Shores of the Great South Bay

I don't know exactly when it happened, but it was sometime during the ninth grade. Suddenly my eyes were opened to a world of opportunities, all of them social, most of them contrary to what my parents thought best. I developed a near terminal case of adolescence, and in the matter of only a year, moved from a full schedule of honors classes to rarely honoring classes with my presence.

In January of my senior year of high school, I made my first adult decision (by which I mean potentially disastrous and legally binding) and enlisted in the United States Marine Corps. I did so not out of love for country or a burning desire to serve, but because the *New York Times* classified section was devoid of any advertisements beckoning the services of a first-class lyricist.

A couple of weeks before, my father and I had been engaged in one of our deep, heart-to-heart talks about my future. Dad decided to cut to the chase and asked the inevitable question: "So what do you plan to do with your life?"

I gave his question serious and heartfelt consideration. Ruling out those occupations burdened by manual labor, constant repetition, or occasional thought, I stumbled across the perfect job. (Those were three of the longest seconds I can remember.)

Confident in my abilities as a guitarist and fond of putting words to music, I responded with the only natural answer and informed him of my intentions to seek fame and fortune in the music-writing business. Dad reacted in typical parental fashion going into shock. Once he stopped sputtering and caught his breath, however, he seemed genuinely interested in my career choice, if not more than a little amused.

"I'm sorry," Dad said, wiping his chin with a napkin, "did you say lyricist?" Dad's hearing started to wane when I entered high school. I often found it necessary to repeat myself three or four times before he grasped the context of an entire sentence.

"Yeah," I responded. "I figure all I have to do is write one or two top-forty songs a year, and I'll be set for life." (With the introduction of disco, how hard could that be?)

Always the perfect father, ready to help when the need arose, Dad threw me the classified section of his daily paper and instructed me to look for "lyricist." "It should be under *L*," he added helpfully, "along with lion tamer and lamebrain."

Now I'm here to tell you that while the *New York Times* is certainly a fine publication and no doubt worthy of its outstanding reputation for covering the news, their classified section leaves a lot to be desired. In nearly twenty pages of advertisements, not one entry even mentioned the need for lyricists or, for that matter, lion tamers. My father looked somewhat less surprised than I did, even though the search was his idea in the first place.

"So now what?" Dad asked, leaving me precious little time to mourn the loss of my chance in the spotlight. "Got any other ideas?"

"Maybe college," I answered. This apparently reminded my father of something funny he heard earlier in the day because he burst out in a fit of laughter.

"College?" Dad asked, once he managed to compose himself. "You know all those college parties you hear about are interrupted by lectures, classes, and assignments, don't you?"

"Well, sure," I said. "At least I assumed—"

"And how do you plan to finance this venture?" Dad asked.

"Again," I answered, "I'm just assuming, but I figured you would pay for it." Another fit of laughter hinted that Dad might not plan to foot the bill.

"Do you really think I'm going to pay to send you off to a four-year party?"

"You always said you'd pay for college," I reminded him.

"I said I'd be glad to send you to college *if* you applied yourself in high school," Dad countered.

"Fine, if you're going to pull that one out of the archives," I said. "I guess I'll just hang around here for awhile."

As welcome as my parents made me feel over the years, my father proved quite adamant regarding my future living arrangements and what conditions they would entail.

"You are always welcome in this house," my father explained. "But there are several ground rules you need to be aware of." No problem, I figured. I'd been living with those rules all of my life.

"First," he continued, "we expect that you'll pay rent." I could hardly believe it! Now he wanted rent for the same bedroom I had slept in for years—*my bedroom!*

"Second, just because you are old enough to vote, doesn't mean you make the rules. While you live under my roof, you play by my rules." The nerve of the guy! Dear old Dad was turning into a third-world dictator before my very eyes.

"And third, you find a job," Dad delivered the final blow with a smile and a clap on the back.

"Come on, Dad," I argued. "I might as well join the service if I'm going to have to live with all those rules."

"Now you're thinking," he congratulated me. "That's a great idea! The military might be just the thing for you—teach you some discipline, maybe a trade."

"Quit kidding around, Dad. You're starting to scare me."

"Who's kidding?" he asked. "Sounds like a great idea to me."

I filled the following days going over brochures from some of the nicest uniformed men I had yet to, or as it turned out, ever would meet. Air Force, Army, Navy, and Marines—a great bunch of guys, those recruiters. They gave every assurance that their concerns lay only with me, not with the needs of their respective services.

The marine turned out to be the most caring of the lot, and since he seemed the nicest of the bunch, wore the coolest uniform, and promised the most adventure, I made the decision to join the Corps.

At this point, I would like to take a short break from the story line and offer this gem of advice to any teenagers who may find themselves reading this: *Recruiters Lie!* Every last one of them! OK, maybe they don't all lie—outright anyway. But when speaking to a recruiter, keep in mind that they have quotas to fill and jobs to do. If they don't do them well, they get to travel to places like Saudi Arabia and play in the sand for long periods of time. Enough said.

When I came home with the wonderful news of my decision, Mom and Dad appeared a tad surprised. "The

Marine Corps?" my mother questioned. "Why the Marine Corps?"

"Nice guys, good-looking uniforms, you know," I offered in my defense. "Besides," I added, "now I'll be able to make my own decisions about what I do and where I go. I won't have to worry about Dad's silly rules anymore."

Dad took my speech very well. In fact he found a degree of humor in it and hardly stopped laughing right up until the day I left for bootcamp. It was that very same day, the day my recruiter picked me up, that I developed an enormous appreciation for the rules my father handed out.

Within seconds of arriving at Parris Island, I learned there were more rules to live by, and these folks were determined that I learn them well. To them I was less than human, if only temporarily. They didn't love me like my parents did and made no effort to shield me from that fact. I truly appreciated my father from that moment on and understood that he based his rules on reason. Much like the rules our heavenly Father sets, my dad did so out of love.

And one more minor, yet not so trivial, point—Dad never shaved my head or sent me to Okinawa.

"A son honors his father, and a servant his master.
If I am a father, where is the honor due me?
If I am a master, where is the respect due me?"
says the LORD Almighty.
"It is you, O priests, who show contempt for my name.
But you ask, 'How have we shown contempt for your name?'"

Malachi 1:6

TWENTY

Life, Liberty, and the Pursuit of Rumors

When I was a boy, and enjoyed the benefit of my grand-father's wisdom, he used to tell me that rumors are like politi-cians: "They're not worth listening to," he told me, "and only 10 percent have any basis in the truth." Over the years, as I gain more exposure to each, I have begun to view my grand-father as less an aging curmudgeon and more a hopeless opti-mist—certainly, at least, where politicians are concerned.

Grateful for the time Grandpa shared with me, and not one to discount the time-tested advice of my elders, I do see some subtle differences between the two that bears further ex-amination. Rumors, for instance, are given birth out of the speech of one or two individuals and quickly take on a life of their own. They leave their parents quickly to make their own way in the world. Sometimes returning, but rarely recogniz-able, rumors change and transform, taking on whatever shape necessary to appear larger than life and more impressive. Pol-iticians, on the other hand, . . . well, never mind.

Through personal experience, I have come to realize that rumors, while occasionally malicious, are often borne out of fear or simple misunderstanding. Falling stock values or a decline in sales may lead to whispers of plant closings or massive layoffs. A misconstrued word combined with an active imagination sometimes brings new meaning to otherwise harmless conversation. Such was the case with the "Great Rumor," the one that nearly tore our neighborhood apart.

It all started when Mary Gianelli, the large and menacing sister of my friend Anthony, celebrated her sweet sixteen. I certainly never begrudged her a birthday, though I found some difficulty in applying the word *sweet* to anything related to Mary's growth or aging process. By general consensus she was deemed the toughest guy anyone knew or had ever heard of.

Possibly out of love or, more likely, fear of retaliation, Mr. Gianelli, not a man known for lavish expenditures, uncharacteristically consented to throwing a birthday party for his only daughter. Everyone received an invitation—by "everyone" I mean, all of the kids her age. I was asked along under the pretense of keeping her brother company and, thus, out of the limelight—a task, I might add, only slightly less challenging than attaining world peace in our time.

Midway through the evening, Mr. Gianelli whistled sharply to attract everyone's attention. "Time for the gifts," he announced, and by the ear-to-ear grin he sported we all knew to keep an eye out for something special. Mary lumbered to the front of the room and grabbed a spot amidst her presents.

Nothing out of the ordinary surfaced, and Mary was unwrapping the last of our offerings when her father slipped out the back door. A few minutes later, Mr. Gianelli returned with his special gift, the result of what must have been several months of serious effort. Solid cedar, resting on castors and tied with a pink ribbon, Mr. Gianelli presented Mary with a hope chest, crafted by his own two hands.

"So, just what is a hope chest, anyway?" I whispered to Tony below the ooohhhhs and aaahhhhs of the crowd.

"Beats me," Tony answered. "Maybe she hopes her face will clear up before she graduates." That comment solicited a smack in the back of the head, delivered with love from Mrs. Gianelli, who had strategically stationed herself to our rear.

"A hope chest," Mrs. Gianelli quietly explained, "is for young ladies to put away special things for when they get married."

"So what's Mary need one for?" Tony asked. That comment drew a second swipe from his mother's hand, but Tony managed to duck beneath it.

"Mary is not a little girl anymore," Mrs. Gianelli informed us. "Today, she is a young lady." At this revelation I nearly volunteered an opinion that might have been worth incurring Mrs. G's wrath, but as circumstance would have it, Tony beat me to the punch.

"And I'm the Pope," Tony said. The resulting barrage didn't seem to bother Tony much, as he laughed throughout the ordeal.

"You have no respect!" Mrs. G. yelled and stomped from the room.

We all left the party that evening quite impressed with Mr. Gianelli's handiwork. Who would have known that it was that very hope chest, the gift of her own father, that started the Great Rumor rolling. I consider myself fortunate to have witnessed, firsthand, most of the statements that fueled this particular fire.

The problem began innocently enough when at school the next morning, one of the girls started telling her friends about Mary's special gift. "A hope chest, you say?" the friend asked. "What does Mary need with a hope chest?" I couldn't help but think how fortunate she was that Mrs. Gianelli hadn't heard that comment. The first girl answered with much the same information that Tony's mom had conveyed to us:

"It's to save things for when she gets married."

I heard nothing more regarding the gift until later that day over lunch recess. The friend who had earlier inquired about the hope chest was in the process of relaying her version of the party (a party she hadn't attended, mind you) to a group of boys. "Did you know that Mary Gianelli's father is already planning for her wedding?" she asked. I found that a strange way to introduce a wooden box into the conversation, but on second thought decided the statement was basically accurate.

After school that afternoon, while flipping baseball cards with a couple of the guys, some older boys walked by, and I caught a piece of their conversation. "Did you hear about Mary Gianelli?" one of the guys asked.

"No," his friend answered, his interest obviously peaked from the tone of his voice.

"Well, I hear she's getting married."

"You gotta be kiddin' me!" the second boy said. "What's she goin' and doin' that for, anyway?"

"I don't know," the first friend answered. "Nobody does."

The match already lit and the fuse burning low, the "Great Rumor" blew sky high with the next and final question.

"Do you think she has to get married?"

"Must be," the first boy answered. "Can't think of any other reason."

Rumors as a rule don't take much time to rise to epic proportions and, for some reason, when those rumors relate to a young woman's virtue they accelerate beyond comprehension. By the next morning, everyone I knew was talking about Mary Gianelli, and not one of them had an inkling of the truth.

By noon, the rumor reached the school staff, and Mary was summoned to the counselor's office as the main attraction in what must have been a very unpleasant conversation. Mr. Gianelli was called in to explain the situation and to get to the bottom of things once and for all. Please remember that this was an era of greater chastity, and the concept of high school girls getting pregnant, while not unheard of, certainly wasn't an everyday occurrence.

From the way I later heard it explained by Tony himself, Mr. Gianelli became incredibly confused almost immediately in trying to decide who he was going to strangle first. Mary was certainly a prime candidate, but she couldn't be harmed until she gave up the name of the boy responsible for this despicable act. Apparently, that only left Mr. Andrews, our counselor and the man who dared repeat such a thing about Mr. Gianelli's daughter. Mr. Andrews escaped mercifully amidst the confusion.

The Gianelli family rode out the effects of the Great Rumor for another week or two as pieces to the puzzle began to fit together and the circumstances of the misunderstanding became clearer. It wasn't long before kids started laughing about how silly the story was in the first place, and it seemed like a new rumor replaced the hope chest almost overnight.

A few more weeks passed and Anthony's birthday loomed just around the corner.

"Hey," Tony said as we walked our way home from school. "My parents won't let me have a party, but they said I can invite one or two friends over for dinner on my birthday. Wanna come?"

"Yeah, sure," I said, wondering what kind of gift my mother would purchase. "What do you think I should get you?"

"I saw these super-cool handcuffs in the window of the dime store," Tony answered. "Why don't you see if your mom will let you get me those?"

"There's already enough speculation about your future, Tony," I said. "I don't think putting you in handcuffs is a rumor you can afford to start."

"Hey, maybe you're right about that," Tony said. "Maybe you're right."

A fool's mouth is his undoing, and his lips are a snare to his soul.
The words of a gossip are like choice morsels;
they go down to a man's inmost parts.

Proverbs 18:7–8

TWENTY-ONE

The Sound of Silence

While people ponder the deep, philosophical question posed to our generation—which long distance company offers the best rates?—Sue and I are trying to figure out if we'll ever get to use the phone again before our children leave for college. And they are leaving for college someday, mark my words.

Our children have suddenly developed something resembling social skills and find it necessary to communicate with anything capable of answering or dialing a telephone—and I do mean anything. Ron spent fifteen minutes whistling into the receiver last week in thoughtful conversation with someone's fax machine. I chose not to ask which party initiated the call, though I have my suspicions.

Teaching our children to talk seemed like a good idea at the time. They were so small and cute back then, and we were young and naive—who could have known. And besides, all the other parents were doing it. It was reasonable, expected.

But now that they're grown, we literally can't get a word in edgewise. We find ourselves rethinking our initial strategy.

"You're the one that wanted them to talk, you know," I said to Sue as the sound of the phone ringing shattered yet another brief moment of solitude. "You never should have let them watch *Sesame Street*—all those vowel and consonant sounds."

"No," she said. "I distinctly recall a masculine figure holding our children and trying to coax the word *Daddy* from their sweet little lips."

Before I had the chance to form my rebuttal, another ring sounded and was answered in stereo by our son and daughter.

"I'll get it," both children yelled as they charged from their rooms in a race to see who could bounce off the most walls and manage to reach the phone first. Ron, the eldest by two years, enjoyed a decided advantage in size and speed; Melissa showed exceptional quickness and mastery in the corners. As they made their final turn from the hallway into the kitchen, Ron led by a nose, but Melissa, her stocking feet sliding across the kitchen linoleum, slipped in under his outstretched arm and snagged the ringing phone from its cradle.

"Melissa!" Ron yelled, "it's for me!" the obligatory response when one loses a race for the phone. Other top-ten favorites include: "I've been waiting for that call" and "It's not for you," all of which imply a direct line of descendency from the Amazing Kreskin or some other self-pronounced psychic.

There was a time when the sound of a phone ringing meant someone was calling for us—Sue or me—but it would be foolish to harbor that hope any longer. Our friends gave up competing with our children long ago. Now the only calls we get start with "Am I speaking to the man or woman of the house?" and end in a request for money.

Our most recent battle on the telecommunications front came as a result of the latest technological advance in our area—cellular service. The kids have convinced themselves that they can't live without it, and most of their spare time is dedicated to persuading us to finance the upgrade.

"We *have* to get cellular, Dad," my daughter begged, holding our old cordless up for my inspection. "Just look at this thing! All you hear is static, and if you're not standing in the right spot, you can't have a decent conversation."

"Do you have any idea what a cellular phone costs, Melissa?" I asked, confident of the answer I would receive.

"That's the beauty of it, Dad," she answered. "They're giving them away! All you have to do is sign up for a year of service."

"And this year of service costs . . . ?" I left the question open for her to complete.

"Just thirty dollars a month, and we get fifty minutes of free calling time."

"You have an unusual definition of 'free,'" I told my daughter.

"Come on, Dad," Ron joined in. "Everybody else has cellular. Why can't we?"

"You kids don't know how good you have it," I told them, pulling an oldie out of my grab bag of fatherly comebacks. "When I was a kid, we had rotary phones, no pushbuttons, call waiting, or speed dial. And I'll tell you something else, when your grandfather was a boy, they had to share the lines. No calling whenever the feeling presented itself, they had to wait for their neighbors to get off before they could place a call."

"They had phones when grandpa was a kid?" Melissa asked.

"Yes, I believe so, Sweetheart," I said, "but why don't you ask your grandfather the next time you see him, just to be sure?"

Sue and I made a command decision to put the cellular on hold for now, at least until the prices come down or we lose control of our faculties and give in to the pleas and cries of our children. But we still haven't solved the underlying problem; namely, how to manage our existing phones so that we can enjoy their occasional use.

"What do you think about restricting the kids to ten-minute conversations?" I asked my wife.

"They would rather go without oxygen," she answered.

"Well then, how about an overall limit," I suggested, "Say thirty minutes a day?"

"OK, if you're prepared to handle a full-scale rebellion."

"Then what do *you* suggest?" I asked Sue, hoping that maybe she could solve our dilemma.

"All of our friends have kids, don't they?" Sue asked. "What makes you think that we could get through to them, even if we did have access to the phone?"

A ring sounded in the background again, and a moment later, Ron called out to me. "Dad, it's for you."

"Hello," I said into the receiver.

"Mr. Darbee, my name is Ryan Sharpe, and I'm calling from Political Survey International. I wonder if you would mind answering a few quick questions for us."

"How long will this take?" I asked.

"Just a few minutes, Sir. Did I catch you at a bad time?"

"Oh no, not at all," I said. "It's nice to hear from somebody. So tell me, how have you been doing?"

An uncomfortable silence passed before my new friend responded. "Fine, Mr. Darbee. Really, if I'm calling at a bad time, I can try again later."

"No, please," I said, "You couldn't have called at a better time. Go ahead and ask your questions."

Melissa came into the room and gestured toward the telephone. "Dad, can you get off the phone? I need to call Sarah."

"I'm sorry, Sweetheart," I said, "I'm going to be on the phone awhile with my friend Ryan."

"Mr. Darbee," the voice came through the receiver, "really, if this isn't a good time, I can call back."

"Ask your questions, Ryan," I told the man on the line. "My time is your time."

Do not let any unwholesome talk come out of your mouths, but only what is helpful for building others up according to their needs, that it may benefit those who listen.

Ephesians 4:29

TWENTY-TWO

Scraping the Barn Floor

The summer I spent on my great-uncle's farm is one I will never forget. Nestled deep in the heart of New York's Catskill mountain range, the scenery offered a stark contrast to the asphalt and brick to which I had grown accustomed. Mile upon mile of green rolling hills, separated by an occasional barn and farmhouse, blanketed the countryside. Cows meandered through the pasture, leaving in their wake what cows usually leave in their wake, and thus my reason for being there.

A summer on the farm had been my parents' idea. I was sent under the pretense of expanding my horizons and learning what it meant to be a man. With the aid of a hoe-like instrument (technical term: manure scraper), my horizons expanded all the way to my uncle's barn, where I labored at the task of removing from the floor everything that passed through the cows' four stomachs. I noticed right away that for an animal with four stomachs, there was a remarkable amount of material left over after processing.

What part shoveling cow manure played in my entrance into manhood I never quite figured out, but in all fairness, I must say it did help to narrow down my career choices. Dairy farming was definitely out of the question.

It was in the process of trying to learn about manhood that I started to envy my Jewish friends for the richness and sense of heritage their religion provided. At the age of thirteen all the Jewish boys I knew were bar mitzvahed, a ceremony where, in celebration of a young boy's entrance into manhood, his parents plunged deep into debt in the process of throwing him the largest party in the history of the world. Everyone brought gifts for the guest of honor, few of which contained beef products of any kind and none of which even remotely resembled cow manure.

One morning, as I labored at the monotonous yet deeply fulfilling task of scraping the barn floor, I began to wonder what it really meant to be a man. While my Jewish friends were being bar mitzvahed and my Catholic friends received confirmation, was I being left behind? Did Protestantism provide a rite of passage that I had somehow missed, or was I left to go it alone? These questions left me feeling a bit unsettled, in part, because I wanted to be considered a man, but also because I had received more than my share of fulfillment at the working end of the scraper. I became determined to find the secret of manhood.

Ordinarily, when faced with a difficult question of life or death proportions, I enlisted the advice of my many counselors, known also as "The Guys." Anthony Gianelli, Elliot Pelzman, Artie Castanza—three sage young men whose advice had proved invaluable, if not infallible, over the course of our growing up. "The Guys" boasted a combined life experience of nearly forty years and always stood ready to dispense their wisdom, often before I was aware a problem existed. With four hundred miles separating me from my brain trust, and my only companions busily chewing their cud, I decided on a novel approach. I decided to think this one through for myself.

At the risk of sounding self-critical, I confess that, to date, thinking had not shown itself to be my strong suit. Thinking had put me and a stop watch inside of a 55-gallon drum, on its way downhill, for the purpose of counting the revolutions per minute. I received a concussion. Thinking had placed me in a shopping cart on that same hill, content in the knowledge that the cage would protect me. I received a concussion. Thinking had . . . well, suffice it to say, I received yet another concussion. Three head injuries in the same number of years left few people expecting or encouraging me to think and several praying that I would not.

As I lay in bed that evening, exercising my mental muscle, I began making a list of the men I knew and the qualities they possessed. Age seemed obvious but was quickly ruled out on the basis that I harbored no desire to remain on the farm until I could shave. Employment was another common trait, but I remembered that when Anthony's father was out of work, he maintained his status as man of the house and nobody asked him to sit in the back of the family car. Unsuccessful, but as of yet undaunted, I closed my eyes and fell asleep, thinking about what it meant to be a man.

Awaking the next morning with all the hope and optimism that a new day brings to thirteen-year-old boys, I decided to follow my uncle around the farm and observe his daily routine. Convinced that the secret to my quest lie in the actions of the men around me, I hurried through the still deeply fulfilling task of scraping the barn floor and rushed off to become my uncle's shadow.

I watched as he milked the cows and listened intently to a lecture on why one should never, under any circumstances, attempt to milk a bull. I saw no obvious connection to the task at hand, but the advice was delivered so sincerely it seemed worth heeding. He stacked bales of hay, and I noted physical strength. He repaired a broken tractor, and I was impressed with his mechanical abilities. At the dinner table, my uncle devoured half a chicken, and I witnessed an incredible appetite. By day's end I held a list of facts, but felt no closer to discovering the secret.

Preparing for bed that evening, I felt a little disheartened and began to wonder if the secret of manhood was too elusive for a boy of my years. The information was there, as were the role models, but something was missing—a binding factor, like a string, to tie the loose ends together. I left my room and headed down the hall to see if my uncle could shed some light on the subject.

The door to his bedroom stood slightly ajar, and I could hear him talking, quietly, as someone speaking to a trusted friend. My aunt was still in the kitchen, so I peeked through the opening in the doorway to satisfy my curiosity. Kneeling at the side of his bed, my uncle prayed. He praised God for His righteousness and love, for His unwavering character, and the gift of His Son. He asked for guidance and direction; he prayed for wisdom, understanding, and strength. Over the course of a few minutes, my uncle brought his concerns, his fears, and his thanks and placed them before his Lord. I left before he finished, not from fear of discovery, but out of respect for the personal nature of the conversation.

In those brief moments, I found what I was looking for: the secret to becoming a man. Though I doubt I could have put it into words, I realized that age, strength, and skill had little to do with manhood. Recognizing our dependence on God, establishing a relationship built on His Son, glorifying Him in what we say and do—these are the marks of mature men and women; these are the fulfillment of our time on earth.

I'll never forget the farm and the countryside surrounding. If I have my way, I'll never scrape another barn floor, either. I'll cherish the memories, the summer of my bar-mitzvah, my confirmation, . . . the summer I learned how to become a man.

> *Those who know your name will trust in you,*
> *for you, LORD, have never forsaken those who seek you.*
>
> Psalm 9:10

TWENTY-THREE

The Nature of Things

Early one spring morning, several years ago, I awoke cold and slightly damp to find myself lost in the wilderness of Yosemite National Park. Sue and the kids were next to me, and as I poked my head out from between the flaps of the canvas torture chamber cleverly disguised as a tent, I noticed what must have been several hundred thousand people, all apparently just as cold, damp, and lost as we were.

As I shook the cobwebs from my mind and wiped the sleep from my eyes, it all began to come back to me. I was not lost after all—well, technically I was lost, because I didn't know exactly where I was, but I was the worst kind of lost. I was lost of my own accord. Much as I hated to face up to it, we were camping.

Completely awake now, the particulars involved with my remote and hopefully temporary relocation became painfully clear. After many years of thoughtfully and carefully selecting our family's vacation spots, I mistakenly passed the torch. In a brief moment of weakness I caved in to the pressures of the group and allowed democratic principle to overcome good judgment. The vote favored camping, and camping we went. Mental note: Avoid yielding to group pressure.

Always aware of the need to model appropriate behavior for my children, I made a visible effort to appear elated with our rustic surroundings. I hid from them my disdain for camping and silently pledged to live the life of Grizzly Adams or Ansel Adams—whoever it was that lived outdoors and seemed to like it so much.

"I can't think of a place I'd rather be than right here in complete and total isolation with three hundred thousand absolute strangers," I said cheerfully. "Yessiree, this is the life. None of those modern conveniences to bother us. No electricity or hot running water, no college football to distract us, just the peace and serenity of being out in the middle of who-knows-where, completely alone except for the massive crowds. Well, I suppose we should get moving and go kill us some breakfast."

"Hold on there, Daniel Boone," Sue said from somewhere deep inside the pile of sleeping bags covering the canvas floor. "Just what do you think qualifies you to hunt and kill our breakfast?"

"Quiet down, Squaw," I said, searching for an appropriate instrument of death with which to fell the first wild beast unfortunate enough to cross my path. "I'm a man. Hunting and killing the family's breakfast is what men do."

"Two things," Sue said. "One, if you ever plan on sharing my teepee again, you better knock off the squaw cracks; and two, you were born and raised on Long Island. Aside from roadkill and what you happen to glimpse in the butcher's window, you've never seen a dead animal. As much as I love you, I don't believe you possess the qualifications necessary for the pursuit of wild game."

If you haven't figured it out yet, while she may be a fine judge of character, Sue is not a morning person. Breakfast came that morning courtesy of our Coleman cooler, which saved me the significant effort of hunting down half a dozen eggs and a slab of hickory smoked bacon.

Our morning meal now out of the way, I turned my concentration toward those activities that make camping such an enjoyable bonding experience for young and old alike.

"I think I got most of the pine needles out of my underwear, Sue," I said, "and the kids are almost finished checking each other for ticks." "What's next on the agenda?"

"Nature walk," she replied. "There's a scheduled tour of Yosemite's flora and fauna leaving in forty-five minutes."

"Honey, I don't think that's appropriate for young eyes to see. I'm surprised at you—introducing our children to the seedy side of life—"

"Plants and animals," Sue interrupted. "It's a tour of the local plants and animals."

"Then you should have said that in the first place, Dear," I corrected.

National parks, I soon determined, are very much over-rated as far as bang for your tourist buck. The nature tour, according to the brochure and Sue's faulty timepiece, supposedly lasted only three hours, but I'm sure it was at least a week long. By the end, I started to believe I could actually see the moss growing and the ferns ferning, though the animals didn't frolic nearly as much as one might expect.

Back in the confines of our canvas prison that night, I kind of let it slip that I wasn't thoroughly enjoying the entire nature experience.

"I'm not enjoying the entire nature experience," I told Sue, while the children foraged around the campsite in search of edible pinecones.

"Give it a try," she said. "Tomorrow, we're scheduled to hike up the back side of Half Dome."

"And Half Dome is . . . ?" I asked.

"A very large rock," she answered.

"Sue, am I crazy or simply the only one that views climbing a big rock as the ultimate effort in futility? This is all so unnatural."

"You need to learn how to appreciate nature," Sue said.

"And here we have the underlying problem, Sue," I said. "This is not nature, at least not to me. You grew up in Minnesota, the land of ten thousand lakes and some proportionate number of mosquitoes. To you, this is natural, but to me, it's like being in a foreign land. I need cement, Darling—asphalt, brick and mortar. I need electricity for crying out loud. Do you know what I really need? Let me tell you. I need a toilet that flushes. That's what I really need."

We worked out a compromise for the remainder of our week in the wilderness wherein I quietly, and with the semblance of a smile, accompanied the family on a variety of excruciatingly boring field trips. In return for my good-natured participation, we ate our evening meals at the Yosemite Lodge (a bastion of civilization) and even played a few pinball games before returning to the campsite to enjoy a restful sleep on cold, damp earth.

I think the kids appreciated the balance—the taste of outdoor living combined with a few familiar amenities. I know I did. And it probably didn't hurt them to witness a bit of the old give-and-take in their parents' relationship. Who knows, they could end up marrying someone with Sue's unusual tastes someday and be asked to make some small sacrifices.

Nevertheless, the next year, a few well-placed bribes swung the vacation vote in my favor. We took the kids to New York to see all of the sites: Empire State Building, Statue of Liberty, Times Square—cement as far as the eye can see. Man, there is something wonderful about that city, the traffic jams and the gray hovering haze. I love getting back to nature.

To the rest I say this (I, not the Lord):
If any brother has a wife who is not a believer and she is willing
to live with him, he must not divorce her.
And if a woman has a husband who is not a believer and he is
willing to live with her, she must not divorce him.
For the unbelieving husband has been sanctified through his wife,
and the unbelieving wife has been sanctified
through her believing husband.
Otherwise your children would be unclean,
but as it is, they are holy.

1 Corinthians 7:12–14

TWENTY-FOUR

Skeletons in the Family Closet

Pssst . . . Psssssst . . .

The sound caught my attention as I slumped through the front door one evening, dragging my briefcase and eight of ten knuckles, my usual Monday night routine.

Pssst . . . Psssssst . . . Pssssssssst!

There it was again, an annoying sound like a pest flying around your ear, urgently circling, looking for the opportune moment to attack. I brushed the phantom invader aside and set my briefcase down in its customary spot against the wall.

Pssssssssssssttttttt!

"For crying out loud, what is that?" I said, slightly annoyed and accelerating toward full-scale aggravation. I shot quick glances from side to side, scanning the area for the offending source but catching sight of nothing.

"Shhhhh! They'll hear you!" A desperate whisper replaced the bug sounds and the familiar nose of my wife appeared as the closet door cracked open. "Quick, get in here."

"What are you doing in there?" I asked, more than a little puzzled with the sudden need for secrecy. "We're getting a little old for hide and seek, don't you think?"

She was in no mood for a game of fifty questions. With a firm grasp on my shirt and a half-dozen underlying chest hairs, she pulled me toward her into the closet. Her left hand reached for the knob and quickly, but quietly, drew the door shut behind us.

"Hi, Honey. I'm home," I said, not sure of the greeting etiquette demanded in these situations. "How was your day?"

"Hectic," Sue answered. "How about yours?"

"Typical Monday," I said, "but something tells me it went better than yours."

"Why don't we call it a tie and agree not to discuss it?" she suggested.

"Well now, I'd really like to go along with you on this one, Sue, but . . . it's just that we're having this conversation in a closet, and I'd feel remiss if I didn't ask for an explanation."

"Do you want the long or the short version?"

"Let's start with the short version," I said, "and you can fill me in on the particulars as necessary."

"All right," she said. "Dog, kids, telephone, doorbell." She delivered the sentence staccato, each word emphasized for maximum effect. Unfortunately, the lack of verbs and adjectives made her story sound more like a two-year-old's new-found vocabulary than an explanation of her day's events.

"I'd like to buy a vowel, Vanna," I said. "I am completely unprepared to guess the puzzle."

She filled in the blanks: "The dog made a mess on the carpet, the kids have been arguing all day, the telephone hasn't quit ringing, and the doorbell stopped working sometime after the paper boy came to collect and before the mailman left this note saying he's sorry we weren't home. By the way, you need to stop at the post office on your way home tomorrow and pick up a package." She handed me a pink slip from the U. S. Postal Service.

"I hate to pry," I said, "but that still doesn't explain what you're doing in the coat closet."

"I needed some peace and quiet," she said.

"Honey, if this is how you get your peace and quiet, you're destined for a guest spot on Oprah," I said. "Wouldn't it be more comfortable if you laid down in the bedroom and shut the door?"

"They'd find me. They're smart, you know."

"Smart enough to chase you into the closet, anyhow," I said. "You know, Honey, you'll have to come out sometime."

"I have every intention of coming out—sometime," she said. "But for now, I have my flashlight, a good novel, and a place to sit down," she gestured toward an old milk crate we used to store files. "Let me finish my book in peace and quiet, and I'll be right out."

"What are you reading?" I asked.

"Tolstoy," she answered. "*War and Peace.* I promised myself I'd get around to it someday."

"I'll make you a deal, Sue," I said. "If you'll come out of the closet, so to speak, I'll handle dinner tonight and occupy the kids for a while."

"And answer the telephone?" she asked.

"And answer the telephone."

"It's a deal."

Sometimes I forget how hard it is being a mom. Not that I've ever been one, per se, but I have taken sole responsibility for the kids every so often. A couple of times, when Sue went on women's retreats, I was left to fend for myself. Admittedly, I never let our children chase me into a closet, but the thought of locking them in one (or two adjoining) certainly entered my mind.

Most of us dad-type fellows have it pretty easy when you get right down to it. We get up in the morning, kiss everyone good-bye, and enter a completely different world. We enjoy the interaction of other adults, compete in the Afternoon Grand Prix on the way home, and return to find a family in reasonable order. Our kids don't take us for granted, because we're not there every minute of the day. Everyone's glad to see us, and life is good.

Full-time moms never leave the workplace. They remain on-call twenty-four hours a day and almost never get a vacation. And home-school moms—now there's some gutsy women—they get the added benefits of attempting to impart an education between preparing meals and cleaning house.

That's a tough one for me to grasp, the idea of living where I work. I get jumpy when I spend an extra hour in the zoo I call an office; an entire night might send me over the edge. It was that thought that helped me find an answer to Sue's problem.

"Hey, Sue," I said, back in the hallway now and free of the smell of mothballs. "Why don't I take a long break tomorrow, and we can meet for lunch. You pick the place. I'll call Kathy and see if she'll watch the kids."

"That would be nice," Sue said. "Maybe the years of hard work are beginning to pay off; you're turning into a thoughtful husband."

"Not thoughtful, Honey. Just frugal. I don't think our medical coverage extends to psychological. And, besides, I've got to eat anyway."

"Speaking of eating," Sue said, "what do you plan on making for dinner?"

"Who said anything about making dinner?" I asked.

"You did. You said you would make dinner, remember?"

"No," I reminded her, "I said I'd *handle* dinner. There's a difference."

"So how do you plan on handling it then?"

"Take-out, of course," I said. "I'll go and pick it up, and I'll even take the kids with me."

"Thank you for being so sweet," Sue said.

"No problem," I said, then playfully added, "but hey, rather than lounging around while I'm gone, see if you can figure out what's wrong with the doorbell." I exited quickly, before she sent *War and Peace* hurtling in my direction and waited for the kids in the car.

"Hey, Dad," Melissa said, climbing into the passenger's seat, "we had a really long game of hide and seek with Mom this afternoon. We never did find her."

"Oh really?"

"No," she said. "Will you tell us where she was hiding?"

"Not on your life, Kid. Not on your life. But I have a better idea," I said. "The next time you guys play hide and seek, why don't you play a trick on Mommy? Tell her to go hide and then don't even look for her. Won't that be funny?"

"Yeah!" Melissa said.

It was the least I could do for Sue, sweet guy that I am.

A deacon must be the husband of but one wife and must manage his children and his household well. Those who have served well gain an excellent standing and great assurance in their faith in Christ Jesus.

1 Timothy 3:12–13

TWENTY-FIVE

The Hug Is Sharper Than the Sword

One thing I have noticed over the years is that the masculine world is divided into two distinct camps: those who hug and those who hug not. Due to what I attribute, in part, to too many years of barracks life and more than my fair share of gym locker rooms, I cast my lot unreservedly with the latter crowd and let the chips fall where they may.

In this age of sensitivity and self-examination, guys like me are beginning to get a bad rap for our reluctance to embrace our fellow man. Critics (die-hard, groping huggers) accuse us of every character flaw from harboring fears of intimacy to homophobic anxiety. Neither is the case, of course. We, the unhuggable masses, simply choose to display affection in other, more definitively masculine, ways.

Traditionally, men have always felt more comfortable expressing their feelings for one another in forums where masculinity is left unquestioned—the playing field or locker room, for example. Nothing says "I love you, Man," like the crisp snap of a wet towel in the small of your buddy's back. A sharp jab to the shoulder also shows you care, though prudence suggests developing more than a passing acquaintance prior to exercising a serious shoulder jab. Some guys consider a pat on the backside acceptable, but only if delivered by a member of the coaching staff, and even then some fairly strict guidelines apply.

In an attempt to assist my fellow man, particularly men who share my fear of the awkwardness brought about by physical intimacy, I have endeavored to categorize the various hugging classifications. This information should be guarded closely, less it fall into the wrong hands and ultimately be turned against us. If studied earnestly and properly applied, this data will empower you to quickly and easily recognize high hug-risk conditions, and apply appropriate countermeasures.

The Compulsive Hugger

Possibly the easiest of the squeeze-happy persuasion to identify, the compulsive hugger finds it impossible to exercise any self-control in social situations. This individual lives to hug and believes that he must grab somebody—anybody—upon entering a room. Once spotted and, if possible, tagged for tracking and future identification, the compulsive hugger proves the easiest to avoid, since you know what to expect and can easily escape an embarrassing situation.

One important point to note: Occasionally, you may come in contact with a compulsive hugger of the large and muscular variety. In this case, simply accept the gesture in the nature it was intended. There is no sense in offending large, muscular men, especially when they have their arms wrapped securely around you.

The Emotional Hugger

Emotional huggers may go completely unnoticed until such time when they are particularly moved or overcome with sentiment (Superbowl Sunday or game seven of the World Series, for instance). Understandably taken with the momentous occasion at hand, the emotional hugger immediately gropes around for a victim to bond with and share his experience.

The Malicious Hugger

Hard as it is to believe, some men actually enjoy hugging other men for the sheer satisfaction they derive in catching us off-guard. These men are often of the large, muscular variety and know they can get away with the affront. The best defense when faced with a malicious hugger is to smile, return the gesture, and hope you spoil his fun enough to send him seeking another victim elsewhere.

As an active member of a large, growing church, I run across the full spectrum of men on any given Sunday. Conscious of their feelings, I try not to offend the hug-oriented section of our congregation, but that is sometimes difficult to do without throwing principle aside and allowing myself to become the subject of a warm, friendly embrace. Even our pastoral staff, six devout, mature, hard-working men of God, are divided between the hug and hug-not line.

Our senior pastor, Dennis Henderson, a former Dallas police officer, is not the hugging type. Craig Stonehocker (Children's Ministry and Adult Education), would rather undergo oral surgery than a squeeze from his fellow man. The four remaining leaders charged with the care of this particular flock are known huggers and therefore approached only while exercising extreme caution.

Prior to attending a major men's conference late last summer, I met with Pastor Craig to develop a polite, but—we hoped—effective policy directed at avoiding group grope sessions rumored to be common occurrences at these gatherings. Sharing a mutual concern for the feelings of the hug-oriented segment that might attend, we planned and strategized well into the wee hours until confident we had produced a foolproof line of defense.

"Let's go over it one more time," Craig said, "just to make sure we've got it right. I'll be sitting at the end of the row with you on my left—"

"Wait a minute," I said. "That leaves my left flank exposed to whoever happens to sit next to me. Why don't I sit at the end of the row, and you can sit on my left?"

"We've been over this," he said. "Why do you insist on harping over that point?"

"I know we've been over it, and I am not harping," I answered, "But I still don't see why I'm the guy taking all the risks here."

"Because I'm the pastor," Craig said. "Now tell me how you respond if a stranger approaches."

"I know this one," I said. "I reach out and offer my right hand to shake and firmly clasp his shoulder with my left, straight-arming him and keeping a respectable distance between us."

"Very good. Now you quiz me."

"OK," I said. "Here's a tough one. A guy walks up to you, obviously moved—let's say with tears in his eyes—and with outstretched arms reaches in your direction."

"Got it," Craig said. "I ball up my fist and hold it against my chest to maintain the MSD (Minimal Safe Distance). Am I right?"

"Perfect," I said. "It looks like we're as ready as we'll ever be, I guess."

The conference lasted two days and truly turned out to be a milestone event. Thousands of men from our area showed up to hear God's Word preached and to study its application.

We heard speakers address nearly every issue that concerned us, from how to mentor our children to improving ourselves as husbands. What a weekend to share with sixty thousand men of God; I almost hoped it wouldn't end.

"That was some conference," Craig said as we made our way from the coliseum and back toward our car. "I'm glad we didn't miss it."

"Me too," I said. "I especially enjoyed the part about accountability and building our brothers in Christ."

"How about when the speaker called for all the clergy to come up front?" Craig asked. "There was such an overwhelming emotional response from the crowd that I actually shed a few tears."

"Yeah, me too," I said. And I could feel the tears returning. "You know what, Craig?" I asked.

"What?"

"You're not going to believe this," I said. "But I think I feel a hug coming on."

"Fight it, Darbee," he said, a hint of desperation in his voice. "Don't give in. You can whip this thing!"

"Oh come here, you crazy guy, you," I said and grabbed him around the upper torso.

His arms just flapped at his sides as I slapped him on the back in the middle of the coliseum parking lot. He didn't return my gesture, but you could tell how it moved him. He punched me in the arm before we reached the car.

Greet one another with a kiss of love.
Peace to all of you who are in Christ.

1 Peter 5:14

TWENTY-SIX

One Man's Treasure . . .

I suppose I should have seen it coming, should have recognized the signs, picked up on the subtle hints. But after so many years of marriage, I really didn't want to believe it was true. Oh, she sent all the right signals, I guess. She even threatened a time or two. Maybe I loved her too much, trusted her too completely. When it finally happened—when all that trust was shattered and her veil of secrecy lifted—there was no one left to blame but myself.

I went to bed early, consistent with my usual routine, but rather than falling directly to sleep, I waited. Because of my morning commute, it's not unusual for me to retire before Sue, anyway. I didn't think she knew of my suspicions, but later she claimed she did. In a way, I think she wanted to be caught, to get it out in the open and end the sneaking around.

About an hour later, Sue poked her head in the door, ensuring herself I was out for the night. I heard the fumbling of keys in her purse and the sound of the back door creaking before I rose and followed in pursuit. Stepping into the garage behind her, I caught her red-handed.

"Aha!" I said, in the manner of one who has just caught his spouse red-handed. "So what do you have to say for yourself?"

Sue spun around quickly, startled and off-guard. Following her first impulse, she feigned surprise and pretended to gasp for breath, all the while attempting to hide something in the small of her back. I didn't fall for the clever ruse, and demanded to see what she held behind her.

"It's nothing," Sue said. "Really . . . nothing." Her face displayed only guilt, and shame shown through the facade of shock.

"Nothing, is it?" I said. "We'll see about that. What have you got there? What are you hiding behind your back?"

"Don't make me show you," she pleaded. "Please, can we just go inside and forget about this? Pretend it never happened?"

"I don't think so, Sue. It's gone too far. I'll be seeing what you're hiding there now, if you please."

Slowly, cautiously, she pulled her hand around. I knew what to expect even before I saw it. "Those are my baseball cards, aren't they?" I said, my heart nearly pounding through my chest. "You've been cleaning out the garage again, haven't you?"

"Yes," she said it defiantly, holding her head up high, ready to stand her ground. She had done it, yes, and she was glad.

"And you've been rummaging through my things?" I asked. "I suppose you've thrown away some of my stuff?"

"Yes," she answered, "and I'd do it again if I had the chance. It's all junk. Somebody had to clear it out of here."

So there it was, a turning point, a roadblock in our marriage. We could take the easy way like so many other couples we knew, or we could try to work it out. Our life together was too important to both of us; we had made a commitment, a lifelong commitment.

"We can work this out, Sweetheart," I said, in the spirit of reconciliation. "Let me see it all. We'll do this thing together."

That was one of the most difficult things I have ever done. Sue, like many women, doesn't know the first thing about memorabilia. She sees a box of baseball cards, an old ball glove and immediately heads toward the trash pile. And the whole time our house is cluttered with real junk: photographs, old letters, and hand-me-downs disguised as family heirlooms.

"Show me what you've thrown away, so far," I said, wanting to minimize the losses. She pointed toward a trash can nearly overflowing with my possessions. "Not my first ball glove!" I yelled as I extracted the crown of my earthly treasures. "You couldn't have meant to throw away my baseball mitt."

"It doesn't even fit you anymore," Sue said. "You couldn't possibly get your hand in there."

"But it has Ron Swoboda's signature on the thumb, Sue! How could you do this?"

"I don't see a signature on it," she said, squinting in the poor light of our garage.

"Well, it used to be on there," I said. "You can sort of make it out if you know what to look for." I continued rummaging through the pile. "Now wait just a minute. Do you know what this is?" I asked. "Do you know what you've thrown away?"

"Old baseball cards," Sue said. Accurate guess, but she obviously didn't get the whole picture.

"Not just old baseball cards, Sue. This is Mickey Mantle, 'Mick the Stick,' one of the greatest baseball players of all time. Do you know how much this is worth? I'll tell you, several hundred dollars!"

"I apologize," Sue said. "I never would have thrown it away if I knew how much it was worth. Can we sell it?"

"Sell it! This is my youth we're talking about, Sue. How much is my youth worth to you?"

"How much can we get?" she asked.

Determining that we were getting nowhere on that course, I switched gears slightly and attempted to gain the upper hand. "How much of your junk have you thrown away, Sweetheart?" I asked.

"Over there by the shelves," she pointed in the direction of the washing machine. "A toilet brush that has seen better days, some slippers, and that cookbook your mother gave me."

I couldn't believe my ears. "The cookbook my mother wrote with her own two hands?" I asked. "You threw away Mom's Chronology of Darbee Cuisine? How could you?"

"It's not even a real cookbook, just a list of ingredients," Sue argued. "She didn't write down any amounts. "What am I supposed to do—guess?"

"OK, fine," I said. "Why are we saving this then?" I picked up an old encyclopedia volume and thrust it in Sue's direction. "Open the book, Sue, and you know what you'll find? Dead flowers. May I ask why we are saving dead flowers?"

"Those happen to be the first flowers you sent me," Sue said, as if that revelation was supposed to make a difference.

"They're still dead, Sue," I said. "And quite frankly, I don't understand. Mickey, you toss away without a second thought, and a dozen carnations get immortalized between the pages of World Book."

"Roses," she corrected. "They were roses, and I thought it better to save them than expect to see new ones on occasion."

Immediately recognizing that this, too, was not a course I wanted to take, I changed directions one last time. "Sounds like we compromise," I said. "I'll tell you what, I don't mind if you keep the dried flowers. How's that?"

"Fine," she said. "And you can keep Sticky Mickey if it means that much to you."

"Mick the Stick, Honey," I corrected. "Yes, it means that much to me. Why don't we try to get through the rest of this stuff tomorrow, after we've both slept. We'll get a fresh start.

"OK, and I'm sorry I tossed your things without first considering your feelings."

We headed for the bedroom, hand-in-hand, the disagreement now behind us, when Sue asked another question. "By the way," she said. "What is that tooth you saved in the baby food jar?"

"Tell me you didn't throw away the tooth," I said. "That wasn't just any tooth, Sue. That tooth belonged to Dave Schultze, hatchet man for the Philadelphia Flyers back in the seventies. I picked it up off of the ice after an Islanders game. At least I think it belonged to Schultze. Hockey players lose a lot of teeth, and it's not always easy keeping track and watching the puck, too."

"You took the man's tooth?" Sue asked in a voice that hinted disbelief. "Didn't you offer to give it back to him, at least?"

"Nah," I said. "Those guys drop their teeth all the time. They're like souvenirs. If they really cared about their dental work, they wouldn't be playing ice hockey, now would they?"

"I guess not, but I still think you should have at least offered," she said. "And, by the way, the tooth goes."

"Let's talk about it in the morning, Sweetheart."

"The tooth goes."

"Goodnight, Sue," I said.

"Goodnight."

As we drifted to sleep, I thought about how some people can't seem to appreciate the finer, more sentimental things in life. And for all this time, I lived under the impression that women were the more emotional partners. It's just lucky she didn't find my collection of athletic footwear. I'm sure she would have burned them.

"Sell your possessions and give to the poor. Provide purses for your-selves that will not wear out, a treasure in heaven that will not be exhausted, where no thief comes near and no moth destroys."

Luke 12:33

TWENTY-SEVEN

Holding On at the Top of the Food Chain

A lot of folks regard dogs as wonderful pets and rank them among the smartest of animals, but, as far as I can tell, we didn't get that kind. Rascal, my daughter's mongrel, is a fairly ignorant animal, even as animals go. I doubt he'd fare well in comparison to a hedgehog or a lemming on the sole basis of intellectual ability, and lemmings make a habit of walking en masse into the sea.

Our sojourn into the world of pet care began a few years into our marriage when Ron began talking and pointing, and became absolutely enamored with a neighbor's tropical fish tank. It was cute the way he sat in front of the aquarium an hour at a time, pointing at the swordtails and giggling at their antics. It didn't matter to him that the sum total of their antics involved swimming a never-ending circular pattern. He enjoyed it, and Sue enjoyed anything that occupied Ron for more than a few short minutes.

We soon purchased our own aquatic habitat and stocked it with a pair of colorful, if not hearty, visitors. To call them anything more than visitors would imply that they planned to stay for some duration, which turned out not to be the case.

Decorating our aquarium in an East River/Hudson Bay motif, we spent a fair amount on colored gravel, pumps, filters, and numerous temporary residents who stayed long enough to avoid the title "vagrant," but never beyond the transient stage. A well-placed ceramic shoe and hastily scuttled ship finished off our decorative composition.

"How do these things survive in the wild, for crying out loud?" I asked my wife as I read the instructions regarding the care and feeding of our pets. "The space shuttle doesn't have this many restrictions. We have to keep the temperature constant within six degrees, add four drops of this and six drops of that for every gallon of water, and keep a light on the tank for eight to twelve hours a day. If we feed them too much, they'll die," I continued, "and if we feed them too little, they'll die, anyway." That turned out to be my first prophetic statement regarding our new friends.

Four days later, Adam and Eve—you can thank Sue for the names—began looking a little green around the gills. By day five, Adam restricted his swimming to a modified back-stroke barely in keeping with the tides. Eve seemed content with hovering near the bottom and sending tiny bubbles upward every now and then. Day six found the ill-fated pair floating belly up, no longer satisfied with this world.

The traditional burial at sea, held in our bathroom, called for me to say a few kind words before sending them on their way. "Ashes to ashes, dust to dust, fins and gills, flush we must," I uttered over the burial site. Ron, as the primary owner, pushed the handle and closed that particular chapter.

Our next pair of tropicals met a similar fate, as did the half-dozen others who followed behind them. Within two months, we gave up on fish and decided a mammal might prove easier to care for.

"It's a rat!" Sue said on first inspection of the hamster.

"No, it's a hamster," I said. "Rats have long tails."

"I don't care how long the tail is, it's still a rat." It didn't appear Sue was bonding well with our new resident. "Don't ask me to touch it, feed it, or clean its cage," she said. She didn't mean a word of it though and was cleaning the cage in only a few short weeks.

On the basis of longevity alone, the hamster did pretty well and managed to survive the better part of eight months. She might have made it a year were it not for our failure to adequately communicate with our son. Ron, in a moment of minimal supervision, decided the hamster needed a bath and brought her to the spot we had last seen his aquatic pets. Upon finishing the business at hand, he flushed the toilet, neglecting first to remove what I imagine was one uncomfortable rodent.

Moving up the food chain, our next addition came in the form of a cat. Felines, every bit worthy of their reputation as aloof and independent borders, are never adopted; rather they choose who they will grace with their presence. Puff chose to grace us, and we tried for some time to prove worthy of her benevolent gesture.

Melissa entered the picture during the post-hamster era and prior to the arrival of our cat. Both the children enjoyed playing with Puff, much more so than Puff enjoyed playing with the children. An unfortunate incident, wherein one of my angels wrapped the cat in mini-blind cord, almost cut the relationship short, along with Puff's supply of oxygen. Animal rights activists will be pleased to note that I suffered greater injury than she did during my attempts to free her from her entwined imprisonment.

Somewhere around the two-year mark, Puff met her end at the wheels of a careless driver, though some witnesses screamed suicide, claiming the cat saw the vehicle approaching and threw herself directly in its path. I admonished Sue for spreading that rumor, preferring to keep unsullied the reputation of our unfortunate friend.

That brings us to the current era and our loathsome, though so far sturdy, tenant, Rascal. A Labrador retriever mix, Rascal is the antithesis of Lassie or Rin-Tin-Tin and is sooner likely to start a fire in our home than pull us from the burning embers. Completely void of any redeeming quality save life itself, Rascal passes the majority of time thinking up new ways to aggravate me. Before you accuse me of paranoia and throw around that old argument about dogs being incapable of such thoughts, you need to meet this dog.

After saving Rascal from an uncertain future as the runt of an unwelcome litter, I expected a degree of gratefulness and, if nothing else, loyalty. Dogs are known for loyalty, after all, and I didn't think I was asking too much. These two characteristics were omitted from Rascal's share of the gene pool, however, and what I received instead was tolerance with a healthy mix of disdain.

Rascal developed the habit of chewing everything I own—my slippers, the leg of my chair, and even made a valiant attempt at the front-left tire of my new car. He has instigated his attack directly at me, leaving every piece of property associated with the other family members alone and untouched. The dog has it out for me, and still I bring myself to feed and care for the animal.

For all his faults and shortcomings, as long as he stays alive, Rascal has a place in our home. Obnoxious and socially inept as he may be, he seems to thrive in this environment, outlasting all of his predecessors by far. The kids need a pet they can help take care of, and as for me, I'm just happy he's too big to fit in the plumbing.

"Look at the birds of the air; they do not sow or reap or store away in barns, and yet your heavenly Father feeds them. Are you not much more valuable than they?"

Matthew 6:26

TWENTY-EIGHT

The Handy Man

Men and women are different. I figured this out primarily on my own, and while I do like to avoid generalizations as a rule, in some cases, they become necessary.

Aside from the obvious physical differences, there are a myriad of emotional, spiritual, and behavioral distinctions that set men and women apart. A pastor friend of mine says that we are wired differently, a description that, though simple, describes the variations in terms we men can easily understand.

When Sue and I moved into our first apartment, the differences in our basic thought processes, as well as what we felt was important and why, became apparent and threatened to set the fuse on our first marital disagreement. Consistent with generations of women before her, Sue felt the need to decorate our new home, while I busied myself with the more important tasks at hand like setting up the stereo and finding an outlet for the lava lamp. It was a struggle from the very start.

"What color do you think we should paint?" Sue asked someone, and after several moments of silence, I cleverly determined that the someone was me.

"Paint what?" I asked.

"The walls, Silly! What color should we paint the walls?"

"The walls already have paint, Sweetheart," I said. "Why on earth would we want to paint them again?"

"Because it's our house now, and we should paint it in colors that represent us," she answered.

Herein lies the first and probably most significant difference between the sexes. Much to Sue's surprise, I quickly informed her of a startling piece of information, hitherto unbeknownst to my darling bride (bear with me, I've always wanted to use hitherto and unbeknownst in the same sentence). Men do not have colors that represent us. We have teams that distinguish us, attitudes that define us, even actions that typify who we are, but at no time and in no way do we have colors (aside from our uniforms) that represent us.

Women, on the other hand, can and often do define themselves by color. Sue sometimes chooses her outfit based on her given mood. And I am not implying here that she is moody; I want to get that point across upfront. If the sun is shining, the day is good and everything is right in the world, she chooses something bright and colorful. When things are a little down and maybe not going her way, she sticks to darker shades—earthtones, for example.

Mind you, Sue actually explained this to me so that I could write it down and communicate the message. I certainly didn't notice it of my own accord, which brings me to the second major difference: We guys are not terribly observant.

Actually, that's not quite true. We have the capacity to be every bit as observant as the next guy—or the next woman, for that matter—we just direct our observations at different things.

For example: A few days ago, Sue asked me to stop by the ballet shop in town and pick up a green leotard for her.

"Nope," I said. "Can't do it. I don't feel comfortable buying ladies underwear. Besides, since when are you interested in ballet?"

"I'm not," she said. "I need the leotard for my exercise class. And it's a stocking, not underwear."

"OK, then how long have we had a ballet store in town?"

"It's always been there," she said.

We live in a small town, forty thousand people, and have lived in this town for over seven years. Never once do I remember seeing a ballet store, before or since. In fact, aside from the hardware store, a grocery, and two or three garages, I couldn't tell you what stores do business here. For that matter, I don't know the streets, either. If someone were to call me from around the block and ask for directions, I doubt I could direct them to our home. However, I can tell you on what aisle you'll find machine screws, where the pneumatic tools are located, and the names of every clerk in our hardware store.

Sue can tell you their birthdays and probably give a relatively accurate account of their family histories. The odd thing is she rarely visits the hardware store. She does care about details, though, and takes the time to observe the people around her. We definitely have a different view on things.

Among the things we view differently are appliances. Women see household appliances as tools to be used, and men see them as excuses to use tools on something. To this day, Sue cannot comprehend how I possess the ability to repair the dishwasher, but seem incapable of loading and operating it. She has similar questions regarding the washer/dryer combo and the vacuum cleaner. I can fix them—strip them down, replace the belts, overhaul everything not yet hauled enough—but show absolutely no aptitude for mastering their operation.

Another key difference between the sexes is in the way they borrow other people's property. Again, please forgive the stereotype. I realize that some men are better than others when it comes to returning things, and some women are probably just as bad as the worst men. But from past experience, I'd prefer to lend something to a woman—I'd certainly never loan my tools to someone like me.

Case in point: I stopped by my neighbor's house the other day to borrow a pipe wrench. A good pipe wrench costs about forty dollars, which is a reasonable expense if you're a plumber but borders on poor stewardship if you're not. Regardless, I'd much rather borrow Jerry's pipe wrench than have people calling me a spendthrift.

"Can I borrow that two-inch pipe wrench of yours?" I asked.

"Sure," he said, "I haven't used it since the last time you borrowed it."

We searched Jerry's garage for nearly an hour before determining that we weren't going to find the wrench. "You know what, Jerry?" I said. "Nothing bothers me more than coming over to borrow a tool and finding that it's not in its proper place. You really need to get a handle on this garage." He accepted the admonishment pretty well, apologizing for not keeping better track of his belongings.

"By the way, are you sure you returned the pipe wrench after you borrowed it the last time?" Jerry asked.

"Of course I did," I told him. "As a matter of fact, I distinctly remember walking over here and handing it to your son James."

"That explains it," Jerry said. It's probably somewhere in the backyard nearly rusted through. I'll talk to James and get to the bottom of this. Give you a call when I find it."

"No problem," I said.

When I got home, lo and behold, I found Jerry's pipe wrench at the bottom of a pile on my workbench. It's funny how tools mysteriously find their way to the exact location they are needed. Once I cleared the drains, I went right back over there and explained the situation to Jerry.

"You've got more problems with that boy of yours than you realize," I explained. "The little bugger snuck back into my garage sometime after I returned this and put it on my workbench."

"You don't say."

"Don't come down too heavy on the boy, Jerry," I said. "He's just a kid."

If Sue had borrowed Jerry's pipe wrench you can believe it would have been returned promptly. In fact, Sue would have washed the pipe wrench first (something Jerry might not fully appreciate) and sent a thank-you card, and maybe a dozen cookies.

All things considered, I think I appreciate the differences between men and women, but I'm glad to be a man, all the same. I may not remember my own mother's birthday, and I gave up trying to figure out which fork belongs in my salad a long time ago, but nobody expects me to look good in a green leotard, either.

"Give to the one who asks you, and do not turn away from the one who wants to borrow from you."

Matthew 5:42

TWENTY-NINE

Free Moments

Something wasn't quite right. An eerie feeling overtook me as I fidgeted uncomfortably in my recliner and tried to identify the source of the problem. I couldn't put my finger on it; but it was there, and I sensed it. Somewhere, somehow, something just wasn't the same.

I sniffed the air for signs of smoke—nothing. Pulling the curtains aside, I checked the driveway—our car still sat in front of the garage. Suddenly, a thought came to me, and I stopped dead in my tracks to listen. There it was—silence. We don't experience silence in our home often, and when we do, it pays to stay alert and identify the root causes. Parents don't like to get caught off-guard.

Sue came into the living room and started to speak, but I motioned her to be quiet. "Listen," I whispered.

"What? What is it? I don't hear anything," she whispered back in my direction.

"That's just it," I said, "nothing. No arguing, no dribbling basketballs, no herds of children rampaging through the house, I don't get it. What's wrong?"

"Oh that," she said, visibly relieved. "For a minute, I thought something was wrong." Sue apparently didn't share my fear of silence. "I was about to come and tell you that we have the afternoon to ourselves."

"This is some sort of sick joke, isn't it?" I said. "You're going to build me up and then spring some bad news on me. Melissa isn't having another slumber party, is she?"

"Nope, no slumber party and no bad news," Sue said, coming closer and hanging her arms around my neck. "Just a nice quiet afternoon alone—the two of us." I thought I recognized the glint in Sue's eye, the amorous smile, the way she threw her hair back away from her face. Some time had passed since the last opportunity of this type presented itself. I knew exactly what she had on her mind.

"Are you thinking what I'm thinking?" she asked, her smile even more amorous, her eyes even glintier.

"Could be," I answered, raising my eyebrows and waiting her out, not wanting to get my signals crossed and appear too anxious. "Are you thinking what I'm thinking?"

"I think so," she said. "But it's the middle of the afternoon. I'd feel kind of funny."

"We're adults, Sweetheart. It's nobody's business but our own."

Dropping her arms from around my neck, she grabbed my hand and we scurried off into the bedroom, Sue giggling like a schoolgirl the entire length of the hallway.

"Should I set my alarm clock, or do you want to set yours?" I asked. "And how long before the kids get home?"

"Go ahead and set yours," she said. "Ron's over at Eric's house playing chess, and Melissa went to the movies with Sarah. We have at least two hours."

I climbed into bed and reached over to kiss my wife. "Pleasant dreams, Sweetheart," I said. "See you in a couple of hours."

"Goodnight," she answered. She must have been awfully tired, because she mumbled unintelligibly for several minutes before finally drifting off to sleep.

There is something about an afternoon nap that brings a new perspective to an otherwise hectic day. When we awoke, I felt rested and refreshed, though Sue appeared a bit on the cranky side. I guess some people shouldn't sleep in the middle of the day. I remembered a little surprise I stored away earlier, hidden deep in one of the kitchen cupboards and offered to share my bounty. "You know what would make this day perfect?" I asked.

"What?" Her mood was already improving and a hint of the former glimmer returned to her eyes.

"Chocolate," I said. "I stashed a whole bag of those miniature chocolate bars in the cabinet with the pots and pans."

"Sure, why not," Sue said, and none too enthusiastically. I don't remember her ever being so temperamental.

As we rummaged through the cabinets, trying to find my horde of candy, Sue became suddenly reminiscent and began talking about the early days of our marriage. "Do you remember what life was like when it was just the two of us?" she asked.

"Boy, do I. We didn't have to hide the goodies, for one thing," I said. "And we had more money to spend on luxuries. We bought the good stuff back then. Do you remember those truffles I used to pick up on my way home from work?"

"Will you please climb down off the chuck wagon for a minute?" Sue said. "I'm not talking about food. I'm talking about quality time—you and me. It's been ages since we enjoyed any time alone. We could use a weekend to ourselves."

"Tahoe is nice this time of year," I said. "It's only a few hours drive into the mountains. If we could arrange something for the kids and I can swing a few days off from work, I don't see why we couldn't spend a few days alone."

Sue was a sight to see. I've seen roller coasters with less ups and downs than she displayed that afternoon, and suddenly she appeared excited again. "Tahoe? Really?" she asked. "Do you mean it, just the two of us?"

"Sure, Sue," I said. "We deserve a break from time to time. Every couple needs to get away once in a while and enjoy a little quiet time."

She ran around the house combing the drawers for brochures and magazine advertisements almost before I finished the sentence. Within a few short minutes, Sue collected an assortment of pamphlets from the Lake Tahoe area, a restaurant guide to the Sierra Mountains, and the telephone number of the Tahoe Chamber of Commerce.

"Where do you think we should stay?" she asked, excited as I've seen her for quite some time. "We could rent a small cabin in the woods, something rustic and romantic, or we could stay in one of the big hotels and pamper ourselves with room service. It doesn't matter to me, you make the choice."

It just so happened that I knew exactly where I wanted to stay. "Have anything there on the Resort at Squaw Creek?" I asked. "I've heard great things about Squaw."

Sue rifled through the brochures like a mad woman, but didn't come up with anything on Squaw Creek. "I don't think so, Honey," she said. "Tell me about it. Do they have a four-star restaurant, hot tubs in the rooms, gazebos by the lake? I can't believe we're really going to do this. Where did you hear about this place?"

"I don't know if they even have a restaurant," I said, "but one of my golf magazines rated their course among the best in Northern California. You remember Lee Mangum, don't you?" I asked. "Well, he took a job up there as the assistant superintendent for the grounds. He claims it's some of the best golfing around."

Sue's roller coaster began another down-hill climb right about then, which surprised me because I thought she always liked Lee and Lori Mangum. She tossed the handful of papers on the counter and stormed into the next room.

Following along behind her, I inquired as to the cause of her sudden loss of enthusiasm.

"I don't even play golf," Sue said. "I thought we were planning a weekend for the two of us."

"You don't have to play the game to enjoy the scenery," I said. "The point is we'll be alone together for a few days. Hey," I said, in my most conciliatory voice, "you can caddie for me if you want to and we'll spend every minute together."

A sudden change of heart came over Sue, and she decided a weekend away wasn't such a great idea, after all. It can be awfully difficult trying to figure out what she wants sometimes.

The kids arrived home at about the time our conversation ended and another thought struck me. "You know, Sue, I was just thinking," I said. She admitted to more than mild surprise at that revelation, and I hadn't even gotten to the main point yet. "All this talk about spending time together and getting away for a weekend reminds me of another area that's suffered a bit," I continued. "We may have neglected the physical side of our relationship lately. The next time we have the house to ourselves, we should take better advantage of the situation."

Back to her old self again, Sue walked to where I stood, raised her foot, and playfully crushed my instep with her heel. "Why that's a wonderful idea," she said through clenched teeth. "Why didn't I think of that?"

"Don't be so hard on yourself, Sweetheart," I said. "I just thought of it myself."

The wife's body does not belong to her alone but also to her husband. In the same way, the husband's body does not belong to him alone but also to his wife. Do not deprive each other except by mutual consent and for a time, so that you may devote yourselves to prayer. Then come together again so that Satan will not tempt you because of your lack of self-control.

1 Corinthians 7:4–5

THIRTY

Code Name "Joshua"

Silhouetted by the soft, dim glow of the morning's first rays, Agent Joshua hurried about the business at hand, preparing to leave the safety of his home station for the uncertainties of life on assignment. Making the final checks of his equipment, he stood before an open briefcase and surveyed its contents.

Notepad—*check*
Business cards—*check*
Pocket Bible (small and discreet)—*check*
Bag Lunch—*check*
Pager—*check*

Satisfied with the preparation, Joshua closed the briefcase and departed for what he hoped would prove an uneventful day in the enemy camp. Moments later, behind the wheel of a conservative American-made commuter, he drifted quietly and unnoticed into the heavy flow of rush-hour traffic, bound for uncertainty in a world gone bad.

Alan Johnson, code name "Joshua," allowed his mind to wander as he switched between lanes, weaving through the line of nameless vehicles piloted by nameless men. Completely anonymous, no little fish decal or pithy bumper sticker to testify his faith, he traveled hastily down a familiar and comfortable road.

Some time had passed since he last spoke to the boss, "JC" the guys at the agency called him. *I should establish contact again, soon,* he thought. *Check in, let him know what I need.*

Arriving safely at his destination, Agent Joshua stopped the vehicle neatly between the lines of his customary parking space and set the hand brake firmly. He was ready, prepared—equipped for the assignment he laid out for himself: low-key saint, cloak-and-dagger Christian, covert operator for Christ.

Alan knew there must be other operatives at work in his location, men and women of God quietly scoping out the territory, collecting data, waiting for opportune moments to make their moves. Certainly the boss hadn't sent only him. Though try as he might, he couldn't identify another agent. They were good—very good. Nobody working with Alan suspected that Christians had infiltrated their place of business. No outward signs existed, no careless evidence left to convict.

Closing the door of his office behind him, Alan quickly surveyed his surroundings. Blinds drawn, door securely locked, he breathed a sigh of relief and placed his briefcase on the desk before taking his seat at the work station. Agent Joshua extracted the tiny pocket Bible and carefully surrounded God's Word with several financial reports—decoys should anyone happen to bypass the security efforts and come upon him. Thumbing randomly through the volume, as was his habit, he paused at 2 Timothy and began reading his selection of the day.

"So do not be ashamed to testify about our Lord, or ashamed of me his prisoner. But join with me in suffering for the gospel, by the power of God," he read. The verse couldn't have been meant for him, he thought as he quickly rifled the pages and chose an alternate selection. "Dumb luck, coincidence—that's all it is," he mumbled.

Stopping next in the book of 1 Peter, fourth chapter, Alan's eyes came to rest on the sixteenth verse: "However, if you suffer as a Christian, do not be ashamed, but praise God that you bear that name."

"No!" he yelled, and then remembering where he was, he repeated it quietly, "No." Hands clasped and eyes shut, Alan bowed his head and attempted to reopen communications with the boss. "This can't be Your will," he uttered in a hushed, subdued tone. "You know what happens when we're exposed. You can't mean for that to happen to me." Alan felt a churning in his stomach, the gnawing of guilt, the pangs of conviction.

"I won't do it; I can't do it," Alan said, and abruptly broke off the conversation, even before waiting to receive an answer.

Agent Joshua knew only too well what happened to those who blew their cover. He saw it happen on his last assignment, when he worked in the satellite office across town. Oh, everything appeared acceptable at first—friendly smiles from the coworkers, nods in the hallway—they were tricky those unbelievers. But they eventually attacked the careless saints, and they would attack him, just the same.

The moment a Christian let down his guard and dropped the protective mask of worldliness, critics swarmed from the woodwork. Once respected and productive members of the workforce became social outcasts, ostracized from the employee community, cut off from their old society. People approached them with caution, stopped telling jokes that might offend, and didn't invite them to parties. Then the offhand comments followed, former friends snickering behind their backs, names like "holy roller," and "religious nut." No, Alan didn't intend to go down like that.

"Pull me in, boss," Alan said, making one last attempt at communication. "Pull me in. I'd rather take another assignment than end up like that." Paging through his instruction manual yet again, Agent Joshua stumbled across the following verse:

"'For whoever wants to save his life will lose it, but whoever loses his life for me and for the gospel will save it'" (Mark 8:35).

Alan Johnson's head dropped to the top of his desk as silent tears welled toward the surface. He cried noiselessly, his entire body shuddering, as he feared the implications of a decision he lacked the strength to make.

Sometimes the world appears filled with secret agents, clandestine Christians, spies for the Lord and Savior Jesus Christ. I say that apologetically more than accusingly, accepting a healthy portion of the blame for myself. There was a time when I bought in to the very same lie and convinced myself of the need for discretion. Hiding behind a facade of management liability, I reasoned that by actively sharing my faith with those I worked with, I exposed my employer to potential litigation.

"I didn't get a raise because I refused to visit his church," I imagined an employee saying. "He'll never promote me because I'm a Mormon," or "The Christians get all of the good assignments," were the words I expected to hear. Witnessing is more than speaking; I reasoned, it is how we live our lives. If I live like a Christian, won't people see Christ at work within me? I can be just as effective in an action-based, nonverbal way and save the conversation for off-work hours. Wrong.

Was I too cautious? Definitely. Nobody was receiving any raises, promotions, or for that matter, good assignments, so what was I worried about anyway? No, my excuses stemmed more from my own fear of rejection than from any threat to my employer. And as God often does, He soon placed me in a situation where my choices became clearer, black and white—a "put up or shut up" situation.

I wandered into the supply area one morning and noticed that Ernie, our inventory specialist, appeared somewhat distressed. Usually a friendly, talkative guy, Ernie was certainly worried about something. His head hung down and his speech was slow and quiet.

"Hey, what's up, Ernie?" I said, as chipper as I can be before noon. "You look like you've been run over by a truck or something."

"Oh, nothing," he said, "just some personal stuff." His demeanor wasn't improving, and I truly became concerned.

"Are you going to be all right, guy?" I asked. "Is there anything I can do to help?" (This should gain some recognition as a key question not to ask when one attempts to avoid witnessing.)

"I'll be fine," he said. "There's nothing you can do about it. We just found out yesterday that my wife has a few problems and she needs to go in for surgery right away."

"I'm sorry to hear that," I said. And the thought hit me like a freight train: Here was an opportunity to witness, maybe more like a responsibility. I could walk away from Ernie and send his wife a "Get Well" card, or I could do what God expected me to do and share the source of all hope. I pulled up a chair next to him and asked if he wanted to talk about it.

Ernie went on for several minutes, filling me in on the details of his wife's medical problem. They hadn't been married long (how come I didn't know that?) and lived thirty minutes away—just six blocks from my house (I didn't know that, either). By the time he finished, God's purpose and my presence for being there were clear, at least I finally thought so.

"You know what, Ernie," I said. "I'm going to pray for you and for your wife, because I know it will help. Now let me tell you something else I think you'll like to hear." I pulled out my small, discreet pocket Bible and started taking Ernie for a walk down the Roman Road—the plan of salvation. After only two steps, my initial fears seemed justified as Ernie held up his hand to interrupt.

"Ron, are you going to tell me about Jesus?" Ernie asked.

"Well, I had sort of planned to," I said, convinced I was staring directly into the face of rejection. "Let me guess, you're not interested." Ernie began to chuckle and quickly allowed the sound to grow into an all-out belly laugh. I chose to refrain from the laughter, however, another emotion began to grow in my own belly.

"Thank you, Ron," he said, trying hard to control his cackling. "But I'm already a Christian. We attend Grace Community Church, and I disciple men in a prison ministries program."

"You're kidding me," I said with more surprise than Ernie appreciated.

"What do you mean, I'm kidding you? Am I that bad of an example?" he asked.

"No, no," I assured him, "but we've worked together for years, Ernie. You would think this subject might have come up before."

"I guess we're just a couple of closet Christians," he said. "Kinda makes you feel embarrassed, doesn't it."

"Maybe even a little ashamed," I agreed. "I think we need to do something about this."

And we did. Over the course of a few weeks, Ernie and I ferreted out a handful of Christian men, all doing deep-cover work for the Lord Jesus Christ. It surprised us both to know how many men believed but lacked the faith to turn those beliefs into action. We started meeting during our lunch breaks every Wednesday in an empty conference room. Our group soon grew to six and eventually ten regular attendees.

Did we catch some flack? Sure. Some people made comments about the inappropriateness of bringing our religion into the workplace. One gentleman even attempted to use it as leverage when faced with a poor appraisal. But one thing I've noticed that bears sharing: It's often the people that complain the loudest and disapprove the hardest who truly want to know God. If we chose to remain silent, we deny them an opportunity He intends for them to have.

As for Agent Joshua, he eventually came around too.

Alan Johnson raised his head and, grabbing a tissue, dried the residue of tears from around his eyes. The boss didn't know how much he was asking, couldn't possibly understand what this meant. Establishing communications for one last-ditch effort, he bowed down and kneeled in front of his desk. "Lord," he said. "I can't do what You appear to be asking. I'm weak; I know that. But You have to understand, I just don't have the strength of character to handle this right now. Please help me, Lord. Show me another way."

Agent Joshua opened his Bible and read his last verse of the morning:

"I can do everything through him who gives me strength" (Phil. 4:13).

He rose from his knees and raised the blinds on the windows, unbolted the door, and set the Bible down in full view on top of his briefcase. With only a few minutes left before the official start of his workday, Alan resigned from the Secret Service and began to formulate a plan—a real plan of action.

"You are the light of the world. A city on a hill cannot be hidden.
Neither do people light a lamp and put it under a bowl.
Instead they put it on its stand,
and it gives light to everyone in the house."

Matthew 5:14–15

THIRTY-ONE

Just a Family Tradition

I think you want to put that over there," my father said, referring to a claw hammer I was about to hang above my workbench. "You're right-handed, and it'll be easier to reach if you hang it to the right." Mom and Dad were visiting the West Coast on their annual junket to see the grandkids. Driving me insane, while not listed on their official itinerary, was an added bonus that came free as part of the package deal.

"That's OK, Dad," I said. "I like it on the left."

"But if you leave it on the left, you're going to be reaching across your body every time you want to hammer something."

I sensed a growing desire to hammer something right then and there but refrained and tried to control my temper. "Dad, follow me on this for a minute," I tried to explain. "There's only so much wall space. Right-handed or left-handed, it really doesn't matter. I can't hang everything on the right side of the bench."

"I realize that, Son. I'm not an idiot. But your claw hammer is a high-use item, and it should be within easy reach. Part of setting up a workbench is making it comfortable to use. You want to design it for minimum wasted motion."

"What are you, an ergonomics professor, now?" I asked. "I like my hammer on the left and on the left it will go."

"Fine, you put it wherever you want, what do I know anyway? I'm just your father." He stomped out of the garage and into the backyard, pouting and mumbling all the way.

"OK, Dad, you win!" I yelled after him. "The hammer goes on the right. Look! I'm putting the hammer on the right side of the workbench. That's where it belongs; I was wrong!"

My father and I love each other very much, and we enjoy spending time together. We play golf whenever we can, board games with the family, or just sit around and talk. But for some reason, among our many traditions (like sharing a can of anchovies or shooting a round of HORSE), we've established a practice of engaging in one ridiculous argument per visit, no more and no less. Neither of us like to argue, and I don't know why it happens, though I'm sure even a mediocre psychology student could have a field day explaining it to us.

Last year we quarreled over the speed I drove Dad's rented car. The fourth or fifth time he told me to slow down, I politely offered to let him take the wheel. "Would you like to drive?" I asked. Mom and Sue were in the back seat cringing, aware of the tension building before them.

"No, I don't want to drive," my father said. "You're doing fine. You just need to slow it down some."

"The speed limit is sixty-five, Dad," I said.

"That's a limit," Dad said, "not a requirement. Just because they post it at sixty-five, doesn't mean you have to drive like the rest of the maniacs on the road." He pointed out an example of one such maniac who just happened to be a highway patrolman. I thought it better not to point that out.

Rather than bore you with the tedious details that were the remainder of our conversation, I'll say that I eventually pulled off to the side and let Dad take control of the vehicle. It wasn't a pleasant outing.

Unlike Dad and me, my mother absolutely detests controversy of any kind. She cannot stomach even mild disagreement and becomes visibly upset when two people argue. My father used to enjoy watching a television show called "Point-Counterpoint," where the political and social issues of the day became the topics of heated debate. One of the show's hosts argued the liberal viewpoint, while the other host stood the conservative ground. I kid you not, the program literally upset my mother to the point of tears. (Once again, probably an easy diagnosis for any run-of-the-mill psychology major.)

With only a month separating us from my parents' next visit, I thought it sensible to speak to my father and, for my mother's sake, see if we could come to an understanding before their arrival.

"Let's make a list," I said while I had him on the phone, "of topics we agree not to discuss when you're here. That way, we significantly reduce the chance of arguing."

"Good idea," he said. "What don't you want to talk about?"

"I don't know, Dad. I guess politics would be a good start. We never seem to agree in that arena."

"That's because you have so many radical views," he said.

"Actually, Dad, it's you who holds the radical views," I said, remembering my old Political Science course work. "My ideas might be confused by some as reactionary, but they are in no way radical."

"Callous conservative," he said into the phone.

"Bleeding-heart liberal," I rebutted.

With the threat of politics behind us, we moved into the next challenging arena.

"Child-rearing philosophies," I said. "Let's agree to avoid discussing how we raise the kids."

"I agree totally," my father answered. "I'm beginning to see evidence of some major flaws in the methods your mother and I employed."

"Don't worry, Dad, I've been able to cover up most of those mistakes."

"Do I get a chance to add anything, or is this list solely your creation?" he asked.

"By all means, Father," I said. "I place great value on your opinions."

"Well then," Dad said. "Let's put physical exams right up there on top."

"Do you mean to tell me you still haven't gotten a physical, Dad? For crying out loud, are you waiting for the coroner to stop by before you plan to see a doctor?"

"I'll go to the doctor when I need a doctor," he said. "You just add it to the list and let me worry about my health."

"Dad, this is silly," I said. "It's been fifteen years since you had a complete medical examination. Would you at least go for Mom's sake?"

"The list, Boy, put it on the list."

"OK, Dad. Anything else?"

"Merle Haggard, Conway Twitty, and Hank Williams Sr.," he said. "You can say anything you want about old Hank's kid, but I don't want you bad-mouthing the father."

"I'll tell you what, Dad," I said. "I won't talk about country music at all if you promise to leave your eight-track tape player at home. Is it a deal?"

"Deal."

Four weeks later, we met my parents at the airport for the start of their much-anticipated visit. It would be nice to spend some time with them; three thousand miles is too great a distance to separate a family. After retrieving their bags from the luggage carousel, we fought through the crowds in the terminal and made our way to the car.

After placing their bags in the trunk, I took my position behind the wheel, with Dad in the passenger seat, Mom and Sue in the rear.

"Try to keep the speed below a hundred, Mr. Andretti," my father said as we cleared the airport parking lot. "And try not to yell at our wonderful grandchildren while we're here. I know you right-wing conservatives have a lot of pent-up aggressions to deal with, but we'd prefer you tone it down a little during our visit."

"No problem, Comrade Father," I said, turning onto the interstate. "By the way, how are your knees doing? Still giving you trouble? You should have that looked at, you know."

"You just worry about driving this car, and let me worry about my health," he said. "And, Son," he added, "tell me you didn't forget to buy the anchovies."

"I bought them, Dad. With capers, just the way we like them. It is good to see you, Dad."

"It's good to see you, too, Son. Now watch where you're going. Are you trying to get us all killed?"

With that out of the way, I wadded my list into a tiny ball and tossed it in the trash. Some folks will never change, and to be honest, I think I like it that way.

"Honor your father and mother"—which is the first commandment with a promise—"that it may go well with you and that you may enjoy long life on the earth."

Ephesians 6:2

THIRTY-TWO

Shattering the Myth of Male Vulnerability

A friend asked me the other day to share my thoughts on the subject of male vulnerability. "That's easy," I said. "I don't have any."

"Thoughts in general," she asked, "or thoughts on this subject in particular?"

"Thoughts on that subject specifically," I said. "It's a myth, legend, folklore. It does not exist. I don't spend any more time thinking about male vulnerability than I do on other myths like the tooth fairy or tales of conservative democrats."

Of course, that's not completely true, but it is the image we men like to present.

A couple of years ago, I was forced, quite literally, to examine myself and my beliefs and to decide how the whole concept of vulnerability fit with my image of masculinity. One of my closest friends, Steve Souza, a deacon in our church, called and asked to meet with me over dinner.

"Let me see if I've got this straight, Steve," I said into the cordless phone. "You want to meet Jerry and me for dinner at the all-you-can-eat ribs place, and you're buying?"

"You've got it," he said. "Tomorrow night, six o'clock sharp."

"And you aren't going to ask me to donate a kidney, or a liver, or any vital organs, right?"

"Come on, Ron," he said. "You know me better than that. If I wanted someone to donate an organ, do you really think I'd be coming to you?"

"I'm going to accept that remark in the spirit it was intended," I said. "At least I think I am. But I'll be there, Souza, so make sure you bring your checkbook. I'm feeling mighty hungry already."

I swung by Jerry's the following night, and we headed for the restaurant to meet our mutual friend. "So to what do you attribute Steve's sudden streak of generosity?" I asked as we backed out of the driveway. "Either he's turned into one great guy, or he has an agenda he isn't sharing with us."

"Could be a pyramid scheme or something along those lines," Jerry said. "This sort of thing happened to me once before. A guy invited Kathy and me to a party, and when we got there someone was drawing circles on a white board and telling us how to get rich by selling laundry detergent."

"Maybe," I said. "But I don't think so. Steve doesn't know the first thing about laundry detergent, and I can't picture him falling for a pyramid scheme. If nothing else, we'll get a free meal to find out."

We decided to eat before engaging in any serious conversation. That way we wouldn't be forced to turn down the food in the event it did turn out to be some shady business proposition. The three of us made a sizable dent in the nation's steer population, and once full, Jerry and I looked to Steve for an explanation.

"I guess you guys are wondering why I asked you here," Steve said.

"If you don't feel comfortable talking about it, we could come back another time," Jerry answered. "I'm free next Thursday night."

"No, but thanks," Steve said. "I was just wondering if you guys had thought much about man-to-man accountability."

"Can't say that I have," I said. "Can't even say that I know exactly what you're talking about."

"Accountability involves holding yourself answerable to other men for your actions," Steve continued. "A couple of guys, like the three of us for example, might get together on a weekly basis and talk about how we're doing, what we're doing, even why we're doing it. The basic premise is that we support and encourage each other to live godly lives."

"Sounds good," Jerry said.

"Yeah, I don't have a problem with that," I added.

"Would we always meet in a restaurant?" Jerry asked.

"Maybe. It doesn't really matter where we meet," Steve said, "as long as we commit to open, honest communication, agree to keep our talks confidential, and hold each other accountable as men of God."

"Let's do it," I said.

Steve wasn't quite finished covering the ground rules, though. "There is one more thing," he said. "It's imperative that we allow ourselves to show some vulnerability. If this is going to work, if we are really going to see an impact, we have to promise to share our innermost feelings, open ourselves up, say the things that weigh heavy on our hearts."

"Waitress!" Jerry called, "I think my friend got hold of a bad rib somewhere down the line. He may need immediate medical attention." Steve waived the waitress off with a sincere apology and an explanation that Jerry didn't get out much and was lacking in certain social skills.

"Now wait a minute here," I said. "I'll have to go with Jerry on this one, Steve. Why—and I emphasize the question—why in the world would we want to do that?"

"To become better men and stronger disciples," Steve answered.

"Then ask me to spend more time reading the Bible, more time in prayer, more time in worship," I said. "But if I understand your idea, you want us to tell each other things we normally wouldn't tell anybody."

"That's right," Steve said. "And that will make us better friends."

"Stands a good chance of making us better enemies, if you ask me," Jerry said. Nobody had, but I for one appreciated his input.

"Jerry's right," I said. "Look, Steve, we're friends because we enjoy each other's company, share a few things in common, and generally like hanging around together. Why do you want to throw a monkey wrench in the works and confuse the whole thing with a bunch of personal issues. Sounds like we'd just be sitting around whining about the problems in our lives."

"And who do you share those problems with now?" Steve asked.

"First of all, I was speaking hypothetically," I said. "I don't have any problems worth discussing, to be honest with you, and if I did, I'd deal with them."

"How do you deal with them now?" Steve asked. The guy sure had a lot of questions.

"I just deal with them."

"Do you talk to anyone about them, pray about your problems?"

"Sure I pray about my problems when things get out of hand," I said, "when it gets to the point where I need some help."

"So then, you handle the small stuff, and save God for the big problems," Steve said.

"Yeah . . . well, no. That's not exactly what I mean," I said. "But I don't bother God with every petty problem and trivial detail."

"Why not?" he asked.

"I don't know, Steve." I began to wonder if the Spanish Inquisition started this way. "I guess I feel like God has more important things to deal with than whether or not I get a report in on time. It almost seems selfish to ask Him to handle every little thing."

"Then God's not capable of handling all of the big problems if He's bogged down with the small ones. Is that what you believe?"

"Now wait a minute, I never said that."

"Sure you did," Steve said. "Just not in so many words. Listen, guys," he continued, "men seem to feel they need to fix everything. Whether it's a car, a family, or even themselves, we don't usually ask for help until we've tried to repair the problem on our own."

"Is that such a bad thing?" Jerry asked.

"Yes, because we're supposed to give God complete control of our lives, depend on Him, rather than on our own abilities. Two verses come to mind," Steve said. "'Pray continually' (1 Thess. 5:17) and 'pray in the Spirit on all occasions with all kinds of prayers and requests' (Eph. 6:18). That sounds like some pretty clear direction to me."

"OK, so God wants us to bring ourselves completely to Him in prayer," Jerry said. "I already try to do that. How is getting all touchy-feely with you two going to make me a better man?"

"Two more verses," Steve promised, "and then I'll climb down off my soapbox. 'Therefore confess your sins to each other and pray for each other so that you may be healed.

The prayer of a righteous man is powerful and effective'
(James 5:16), and 'As iron sharpens iron, so one man sharpens another' (Prov. 27:17)."

"It all sounds good on the surface, Steve," I said, "but I've
got to tell you, I'm a little nervous about sharing my faults and
problems with my friends."

"Why? Don't you trust us?"

"It's not a matter of trust," I said. "Jerry has a key to my
house, and I'd trust either of you with anything I own. If you
want to know the truth, I'm afraid that you might find, in
some respects, I'm not the man you think I am."

"We already know you're not the man *you think* we think
you are," Jerry said, always ready with a supportive comment.

"Jerry's right, Ron. None of us are. The key to this thing
lies in trusting one another with our feelings, our shortcomings, and our fears. It provides a safety net. When we have other men in our lives who care about our obedience to God, we
start to get a handle on the secret sins that eat away at us, and
often go unnoticed. Nothing you do or say will make you any
less forgiven in the eyes of God, or any less my friend."

Our first official meeting occurred the following Saturday
morning, and in deference to Jerry's requests, we met in a local
pancake house. At first, I found it difficult to share the issues
I truly struggled with, but in time, we developed a trust that
is all too rare among God's masculine creation. We never respond judgmentally; the fact is we're imperfect enough to
know we can't afford to.

Whether we choose to admit it or not, men are vulnera-
ble. We share a dependence on God for salvation, sustenance,
and even life itself. Recognizing that vulnerability and acting
on it strengthens every aspect of who we are and who He
wants us to become.

Steve and Jerry and I have discussed marriages and children, health concerns and personal failures; we've prayed for

each other's growth and strength. While I won't say I haven't been surprised at an occasional revelation, I still haven't heard anything that weakened my opinion of these men. I've learned that a man is never closer to God than when he stands on the shoulders of his brothers.

"Hurry up, Ron. I can't hold you much longer," Jerry yelled.

"Just a little to the left, Jer. I can see the ball in the gutter."

"You might try telling your kids not to throw the ball on the roof," Jerry said, as he strained to hold me in position. "You might even consider breaking down and buying a ladder."

"Not while I still have friends like you," I said. He didn't even drop me, such is the depth of our relationship.

Let us not give up meeting together, as some are in the habit of doing, but let us encourage one another—and all the more as you see the Day approaching.

Hebrews 10:25

THIRTY-THREE

Of Things Green and Slimy

There I was, minding my own business, not hurting another soul in the world, about to take the first bite from my double-meat, double-cheese hamburger extravaganza when she stopped in front of our table. A well-meaning, good-natured busybody—self-appointed patrol officer for the cholesterol police, she felt moved to share her philosophy with me.

"Do you know what you're doing to your body?" she asked. She looked at me with that same you-should-be-ashamed-of-yourself look my mother always saved for report cards and conversations with the youth pastor.

"Nourishing," I answered. "Yes, I believe that's the term, Ma'am. I'm nourishing my body."

"You most certainly are not!" she lectured. "You're killing yourself, that's what you're doing."

Sue isn't very helpful in these situations, choosing to ignore rather than confront people who freely express their opinions. But alas, such is not the way of men.

"If it would make you feel any better, I could lie down right here in the booth and you can drive a steak through my heart—rare if you please, with lots of fat." My comment, intended to amuse, neither entertained nor discouraged our health-minded visitor.

"Well if you're not concerned for your health," she continued, "or the well-being of your family," she motioned toward the kids who appeared to be enjoying the conversation, "you could at least show some respect for God's creation."

Finally, a topic I felt qualified to discuss. "Run that by me again, Ma'am, that part about God's creation."

"Every time you eat a hamburger, you kill one of God's creatures," she said. The woman obviously didn't understand how many hamburgers come from the average beef cow.

"I was under the impression God placed animals on earth for man's use," I said. "He expects us to eat them. That's why cows are so dumb and slow. Otherwise they'd be real mean and fast. I imagine that would make them considerably more difficult to milk, now that I think about it."

Persistence not a quality the woman lacked, she refused my attempt to divert her into a whimsical discussion on cattle temperament and held firmly to the original line of questioning. "With all the variety nature offers, why must you insist on eating beef?"

"Oh, I don't know, Ma'am," I said, beginning to tire with the verbal exchange. "I guess because I can't afford veal."

"I hope you choke on that hamburger," she said, and stormed away from our table.

"So much for loving God's creation," I said to Sue as the woman drifted into the distance.

"That wasn't very nice," Sue said, amidst the cheers of "Good one, Dad," from Ron and Melissa.

"Tell me about it," I said. "Some nerve, accosting a family trying to enjoy a simple meal."

"I'm talking about you."

"Me?!" I said, completely unaware of my transgression. "What did I do?"

"You were rude and aggressive, that's what," she said. "Couldn't you just smile and ignore her, instead of engaging in a battle of wits?" After all these years, you'd think Sue could answer that one on her own.

"I'm sorry, Sweetheart," I said. "I realize that wasn't the best example for the kids." The next few minutes were dedicated to explaining to Ron and Melissa alternate ways of dealing with such people.

"You know something, Sue," I said as we were driving home that evening. "Something just dawned on me. That woman in the restaurant tipped the scales in excess of two-hundred pounds, if I'm any judge of size. And I'm not making fun of her, but she didn't get that big on a diet of snow peas and granola. There's got to be some serious animal by-products involved in that equation."

"Maybe that's why she was so adamant," Sue said. "It could be she's battling a health or weight problem and wanted to save you from suffering too." That's one of the things I love most about my wife; she really does try to see the best in all people.

Mistakenly, I thought we shared the last words on that subject, but consequences associated with the lovely woman's tirade surfaced a few days later.

"I saw an article in today's paper that I want you to read," Sue said when I arrived home from work. "It's about the effects of cholesterol and high-fat foods in our diets."

"Let me guess, they're against it," I said.

"I'm not kidding," Sue said. "You should read this." She handed me a clipping from the "lifestyles" section. "We might want to think about changing our eating habits."

"I don't want to change my eating habits, Sue," I said. "Eating tofu and bean sprouts doesn't make you live any longer, it just *seems* longer. Every meal is like an eternity."

"This isn't a joke. We're talking about our health."

"No, you are talking about our health, Sue. I'm just trying to figure out the sudden urgency of a low-fat diet."

"Well, I borrowed a couple of cookbooks from the library," Sue said, "and as long as I'm the one cooking, we're going to try to eat better."

Her ability to negotiate from a position of power was, at that moment, not one of the other things I loved most about my wife. The cookbooks she brought home included: *101 Ways to Prepare Zucchini, Bean Curd, Your Heart's Best Friend,* and *Out of the Frying Pan,* a guide to boiled dinners. Somewhere a deep-dish pizza called my name.

The evening's dinner verified that there was in fact 101 ways to prepare zucchini. What the author failed to mention, however, is that there are only three ways to prepare your family to eat it. They are: Bribery— "If you eat your zucchini you can have some dessert"; Blackmail—"If you don't finish every bite, you'll find it on your breakfast plate in the morning"; and Brute Force—"Eat that zucchini right this minute or else!"

Finishing every last piece of the green, slimy vegetable as an example to our children, I tried to cover the gagging sounds that emanated with each mouthful. Mistaking my good example for approval, Sue offered to send the leftovers for my next day's lunch.

"That won't be necessary, Sue," I said. "I think I'll stop by the cafeteria and grab a salad." (I neglected to mention my salad would be served on a bun and crowned with a quarter-pound of beef.) "What's on the menu for tomorrow night?" I asked.

"Meatloaf surprise," she answered.

I started to salivate at the thought of a juicy, cholesterol-infested meat loaf. "What's the surprise part?" I asked cautiously.

"No meat. You mix two pounds of tofu with the same spices you normally put in a meat loaf and cook it in a mold. The cookbook claims you won't be able to tell the difference."

"Don't bet on it," I said.

For two weeks, not an animal carcass graced our kitchen, and the children began to exhibit signs of rebellion. "I want a pizza, Dad!" Ron said while we hid in his room and shared a contraband beef jerky left over from his last camping trip. "And I don't care what I have to do to get it."

"Give it time, Son," I said. "A couple more weeks and your mother will snap out of it. I've seen this sort of thing before."

"I don't think we have a couple of weeks, Dad. I'm starting to dream about French fries. If you don't do something, I'm going to run away and join a fast-food chain."

"Which one?" I asked, wondering if I might join him.

Melissa knocked softly on the door and begged to come in. "I know you guys are hiding something in there," she said. "Let me in, and I won't tell Mom. I just want a tiny piece."

"You don't even know what it is!" Ron whispered through the door. "Go away!"

"I don't care what it is, but I want some," she returned. "I mean it! I'll tell Mom." Ron let his sister enter and grudgingly turned over a small portion of our bounty. Melissa devoured the jerky like a hungry wolf.

"So this is what we've come to," I said, cleaning the remnants of jerky from between my teeth. "Hiding in Ron's room and sneaking food. I never thought I'd eat anything we found in your room, Son. I promise to talk to your mother. We'll get this thing resolved before the dog becomes endangered. I don't want to come home and find Rascal on the barbecue."

Spending a few hours of vacation time, I came home early the next day to reason with Sue before the children got out of school. A wonderful and familiar smell greeted me as I entered the front door.

"You're home early!" Sue said, surprised at my arrival. "I didn't expect you so soon." Her words were laced with guilt and a hint of Worcestershire.

"What do you have on that plate behind you, Sue?"

"This plate? Oh, nothing really. It's just an itsy-bitsy, teeny-weeny slab of meat. I couldn't help myself."

"And so ends the not-so-great health experiment," I said. "Welcome back to the world of carnivorous dining, Sweetheart. What's for supper?"

"I don't want to go back to eating the way we did," she said. "We should be careful."

"Careful is fine," I said. "Good things in moderation. But no more trying to maintain life on rabbit food and bird seed. Now, what do you want for supper? I'll spring for take-out."

We agreed on pizza, everything but anchovies. Meat, dairy, vegetable, and bread—the four basic food groups. It is possible to compromise and still eat well. A meal never tasted so good.

One man's faith allows him to eat everything,
but another man, whose faith is weak, eats only vegetables.
The man who eats everything must not look down on him who
does not, and the man who does not eat everything must not
condemn the man who does, for God has accepted him.

Romans 14:2–3

THIRTY-FOUR

Getting Around to It

From the start of this project, I intended to write a chapter about procrastination and, appropriately, put it off until last. I tried to write it earlier, even started to map it out a time or two, but never got around to finishing it until the very end.

With all modesty, I consider myself among the world's foremost authorities on the subject of procrastination and would go so far as to say my record speaks for itself. If anyone ever gets around to erecting a hall of fame devoted to the art form, my jersey will hang with great ceremony from a wall in a wing dedicated in my name. Undoubtedly, someone will eventually decide to construct such a hall. Plans will be drawn, a suitable site chosen, and a ground-breaking held to commemorate the event. Finishing the project will prove too grand a task, and the dream will likely die there.

No one sets out to become a procrastinator; we stumble into it. We make no effort to perfect our skills, no attempt to hone our craft. It just happens. The wonderful thing is knowing that if it doesn't happen today, it will surely happen to-morrow.

In this respect, at least, Sue and I differ greatly. I categorize my life by the dates my projects become due and complete them the night before, a sprinter breaking the tape as I dash across the finish line. Sue is the long-distance runner, queen of the twenty-six mile marathon. She looks ahead and determines how long a given task should take, divides the job into manageable sections, and progresses toward her goal one measured step at a time. I find her method very annoying.

More annoying is the resulting free time Sue manages to accumulate. Relaxing on the couch with her favorite magazine one weekend, while I hurried about the task of changing a flat tire that had been leaking for six months, she busily penciled in the answers to a quiz.

"Would it be too much trouble for you to come outside and hold the flashlight while I change this tire?" I asked.

"I don't hold flashlights for you, anymore," she said. "They cause too many arguments. Besides, it's not even dark outside."

"Well, maybe you can hold the jack, then."

"You're just aggravated because I finished everything on my list and you still have that nasty tire to change," she said.

"That has nothing to do with it," I said. "Did you ever think I might just want to spend some time with you?"

"Actually, no," Sue said. "But if that's the case, you can take me out to dinner tonight. And if you ever do find a free minute, you should sit down and take a look at this quiz."

"I don't do quizzes, Sue," I said. More to the point, I don't fill out quizzes found in women's magazines. When we were a little younger, I fell for that ploy a couple of times and don't intend to make that same mistake again. With titles like: "Are You and Your Mate Compatible?" and "Find Your Romance IQ," the questionnaires are a lose-lose proposition, designed to document the perceived failures of unsuspecting husbands. My romance quotient was a three on a scale of one to twenty, for which the writer suggested remanding me to the custody of the local coroner.

"But this one was made for you," Sue said. "It's called 'Gauge Your Procrastination Factor.'" I told her I'd get around to it when I had a chance.

Rather than consider myself a dawdler, I prefer the view that I'm overcommitted. It sounds a lot better to say "I'm balancing too many plates," than "I put everything off until the last minute." The world is filled with men who would gladly subscribe to this explanation, as evidenced by a quick survey of malls on Christmas Eve or greeting card stores on the day before Valentine's.

Sue, like her mother before her, and countless generations before that, rarely puts anything off until the last minute. Her Christmas shopping begins in January and ends by mid-August. My birthday present lies wrapped and hidden at the bottom of her closet three months before we celebrate. She plans dinners two weeks in advance, buys clothes for the kids to grow into, and never allows a coupon to expire. It's difficult to trust a person like that.

On the night before Christmas, several miles from our house, I shop like a madman to find a gift for my spouse. While the stockings are hung on our chimney with care, I'm pacing the mall pulling gifts from thin air. You can imagine how we fared on the compatibility quiz.

We are beginning to see signs of this same behavior manifested in our offspring. Melissa starts sharpening number-two pencils when her teacher announces an upcoming test. Ron, on the other hand, wouldn't study for the bar exam until after he tried his third case, seeing no reason to expend the effort until he is convinced the profession holds some promise for future success. They handle chores with the same conflicting attitudes. My daughter finishes her tasks when assigned, leaving her free to play and enjoy the rest of the day. Ron views the garbage can as a small landfill that would sooner be covered in dirt and left to decompose than find its way to the curb.

"That boy is every bit your son," my wife complimented recently.

"Why, thank you, Sweetheart," I said. "Is it the dashing good looks, or the charming wit to which you refer?"

"Let me know when you're ready to join me in reality," Sue said. "That wasn't meant as a compliment."

"So, what's the problem?" I asked.

"The problem is he puts everything off until the last minute. He finishes his homework at the breakfast table, crams for tests on the way to school, and turns his assignments in as close to the deadline as possible."

"Sounds like a normal, functioning teenage boy," I said. "He always brings home good grades, so what's to worry about?"

"He needs to learn that you can't go through life by the skin of your teeth," Sue said. "He'll be applying for college before we know it, and he needs to develop better habits."

I held no doubts regarding the validity of Sue's statement. I remembered my own college experience, following my discharge from the service. Holding down a full-time job and attending classes at night, the study habits (or the lack thereof) left over from my high school days nearly brought a quick end to my continuing education. "All right," I said. "We'll talk to him about it. Let's find a way to approach this as an improvement, though, so he doesn't see it as a punishment. I don't want to give him the impression we're unhappy with his performance, especially when his grades are so good."

"When should we talk to him?" Sue asked.

"I imagine if I say, 'when the time is right,' you're going to be unhappy," I said.

"How about tonight?" she asked. And so it was settled.

If you knew my son, you would know me. Ron has grown to become the kind of young man I enjoy spending time with, and greater praise from a father you could not hear. He is the son I always hoped for (deserved is the way my mother phrases it). He acts like me, talks like me, we share the same sense of humor (I get to use it until I finish the book), the kid even looks like me. Excepting only his size thirteen feet (we won't mention where those came from), he is in every aspect his father's son. Anticipating his response to our impending conversation didn't prove the least bit difficult.

"But I'm getting straight A's!" was the first comment fired in our direction.

"Slacker," I mumbled and drew a dangerous glance from the boy's mother.

"Your father and I are more than pleased with your accomplishments, Ron," Sue said. "What we're trying to say is you can work a lot smarter, rather than harder."

"Why mess with a good thing?" he asked. "Seems like I'm doing just fine."

"Think about how nice it would be to have your work finished early and have all that free time left over to spend with your friends," Sue said.

"My way, I have the free time in the beginning," Ron countered. "What's the difference?" I, for one, recognized the logic in his statement immediately.

"Not everything is going to come so easy," Sue said. "Eventually, you'll find things a little more challenging, and you'll be glad you learned to manage your time."

"Dad always waits until the last minute," Ron said, "and he does pretty well."

"Now why did you have to go there?" I asked him, knowing that in one sentence the boy had sealed both of our fates. Recognizing the time for my input, I added my support. "Look, Pal," I said. "Mom's right. No one's saying you need to spend six hours studying every evening or complete your assignments two weeks in advance. I realize I tend to put things off occasionally too. So, how about we both try to manage our time a little better."

"What exactly does that mean?" he asked.

"It means that you set aside certain times for chores, certain times for homework," I said. "In turn, I'll do the same sort of thing with my jobs around the house. Let's try it for a while and see how it works out."

His OK came reluctantly, but we took it as whole-hearted acceptance just the same—agreement and acquiescence being synonymous where teenagers are concerned.

"Where are you going, Dad?" Melissa asked as I passed her on my way to the garage.

"To change the oil in your mother's car," I answered.

"Did the engine freeze up again?" she asked.

"No, Miss Smarty-pants, the engine didn't freeze up," I said. "Haven't you ever heard of preventive maintenance? By the way, don't you have homework to do or something?"

"No," she said. "I finished it when I got home from school."

I should have known that. I really should have known that.

"You also must be ready, because the Son of Man will come at an hour when you do not expect him."

Luke 12:40

187